Praise for Steve Chalke and Alan Mann's *Different Eyes*

Every now and then I bump into someone who doesn't 'tell' me how to live my life, but shows me, by living *their* life 'beautifully'. This book gives us an insight into some of the reasons why Steve Chalke is one of those people. Beware, it may well be contagious!

Ruth Dearnley,
speaker, CEO Stop The Traffik

Vital, readable and winsome wisdom that calls us beyond mere goodness to beautiful living. Refreshing and inviting, this is an invaluable tool for us all as we live our faith in the moral maze.

Jeff Lucas,
author, speaker, broadcaster

Also by Steve Chalke

Apprentice: Walking the Way of Christ
(Steve Chalke and Joanna Wyld)

*Change Agents: 25 Hard-learned Lessons in
the Art of Getting Things Done*

*Intelligent Church: A Journey Towards Christ-Centred
Community* (Steve Chalke and Anthony Watkis)

The Lost Message of Jesus (Steve Chalke and Alan Mann)

different eyes

the art of
living beautifully

steve chalke
+ alan mann

 ZONDERVAN®

Oasis
for people & community

ZONDERVAN.com/
AUTHORTRACKER
follow your favorite authors

We want to hear from you. Please send your comments about this book to us in care of zreview@zondervan.com. Thank you.

ZONDERVAN

Different Eyes
Copyright © 2010 by Steve Chalke

Steve Chalke and Alan Mann assert the moral right to be identified as the authors of this work.

This title is also available as a Zondervan ebook. Visit www.zondervan.com/ebooks.

This title is also available in a Zondervan audio edition. Visit www.zondervan.fm.

Requests for information should be addressed to:

Zondervan, *Grand Rapids, Michigan* 49530

ISBN 978-0-310-32680-9

Cover design: Tammy Johnson
Interior design: Sherri Hoffman
Editorial direction: Ryan Pazdur and Bob Hudson

Printed in the United States of America

10 11 12 13 14 15 16 17 • 21 20 19 18 17 16 15 14 13 12 11 10 9 8 7 6 5 4 3 2 1

contents

part one

clear sighted

surprised

God is a common name.

There are thousands of them.

Like countless other common names – Jack or Olivia or Raj or Fatima – there is almost nothing you can tell about the character of any specific god just from the use of that label.

Think about it. Why was Moses so concerned to get clarification as to which god was addressing him from the burning bush?

> *'Suppose I go to the Israelites and say to them, "The God of your fathers ['El'] has sent me to you," and they ask me, "What is his name?" Then what shall I tell them?' (Exodus 3:13)*

El (which in English is translated 'God of your fathers') was a fairly standard way of referring to local gods in the Ancient Near East. Every nation had its collection of gods who were, of course, known to them as the 'gods of their fathers'.[1] It shouldn't surprise us, therefore, that Moses asks the god of the burning bush for some illumination as to who exactly he is. God responds: 'Tell them ... "I Am [Hebrew 'Yahweh']", has sent you' (Exodus 3:14 CEV).

Even today, there are all kinds of names for the gods who are worshipped around the world. And yet, how often do we get into conversations about 'God' and simply presume that everyone is on the same page as we are? How often do we unthinkingly assume that we all have in mind the same kind of God – the God who is revealed and experienced within the story of Israel and the life, death and resurrection of Jesus, the Jew from Nazareth?

The problem is that often people are not only on a different page than we are, they're not even reading the same book!

In *Alice Through the Looking Glass*, in a rather unintelligible conversation with Alice about the meaning of the word *glory*, Humpty Dumpty says this: 'When I use a word, it means just what I choose it to mean – neither more nor less.'

That's the problem with the name *god*. It means just what different groups of people choose it to mean.

But it's even more complicated than that.

If we're honest, exactly the same problem has developed within the Church – there are lots of 'Christian gods'. We have . . .

- the God who approves of war and the God who is against it
- the God who is for capital punishment and the one who is appalled by it
- the God who opposes divorce and remarriage and the God who is accepting of both
- the God who teaches 'Walk with me and I'll make you healthy and wealthy' and the God of those who live in suffering and poverty
- the God who gives us the technology for stem cell research and birth control and the God who is outraged by our development of both
- the God who is against women in church leadership positions and the God who positively encourages them into such roles

Such views about who God is, what he's like and how he wants us to live, not only impact our personal lives and our churches, they even affect the way entire countries are run – sometimes with devastating results.

Consider the Dutch Reformed Church of South Africa, which has been intimately bound up with the politics of the white Afrikaner community. The denomination even developed a whole theology to legitimise its support of the Apartheid system, the institutionalised separation of the South African people according to their race. Indeed, the South African Prime Minister, Daniel Francois Malan (1874–1959) – who led the campaign for complete segregation of the races in South Africa – was himself a Dutch Reformed minister.

What is known as 'Ham theology' made it possible for Dutch Reformed scholars to teach that the Afrikaners, as a race, fulfilled a role similar to that of the people of Israel in Old Testament times.

Dutch Reformed theologians viewed the curse that Noah placed on his grandson Canaan, the son of Ham (Genesis 9:20–27), as the biblical justification for Israel's conquest and enslavement of the Canaanites. Afrikaners believed that black Africans, or 'Hamites' as they were sometimes called, were also descendants of Ham through Canaan.

Their theology also claimed that the Bible accepts racial and ethnic differences – and that this is clearly seen in the story of the Tower of Babel (Genesis 11) and was even recognised by the apostle Paul in his Areopagus speech (Acts 17), where he acknowledges that God has 'determined ... the exact places where they should live' (Acts 17:26).

All this was then used as the justification for segregation and the decisions of white Afrikaners regarding the division of land and their tightly controlled allocation of living areas for nonwhites.

This kind of theology, in fact, was widely held by many European Christian groups throughout the eighteenth and nineteenth centuries, and though it was abandoned by most in the mid-twentieth century, it was not until the early 1980s that the World Alliance of Reformed Churches declared Apartheid to be a heresy and expelled the Dutch

Reformed Church from its federation. Perhaps partly as a result of this, in 1986 all congregations in the Dutch Reformed Church of South Africa were finally desegregated with the church expressing its repentance of 'the sin of supporting Apartheid'.

Is there any wonder that George Bernard Shaw once famously observed that 'God created man in his image – unfortunately man has returned the favour'?

Shaw's contemporary, the influential sociologist Emile Durkheim, suggested that each 'tribe', or society, invents a god who reflects its values, standards, aspirations, hopes, ambitions and attitudes and then worships it – thus legitimising and endorsing its own moral choices and behaviours.

Durkheim has a point. His work is a powerful argument and offers important warnings to us all. The trappings of our culture too easily entice us – and when they do, our image of God inevitably becomes distorted. As Archbishop William Temple once put it, 'The more distorted a person's idea of God, and the more passionately they are committed to it, the more damage they will do.'

What's in a Name?

One of the most significant prayers in the Jewish faith is the Shema – 'Hear, O Israel: The LORD [Yahweh] our God, the LORD is one' (Deuteronomy 6:4).

For literally thousands of years that simple prayer – or statement of belief – has been on the lips of generation after generation of Jews – from Moses to King David, from Jesus to Bob Dylan – it is the first creed they learn as infants, and for many it's the last they utter before death.

Though the Shema is seemingly a simple text, it contains a depth of theology, with its chief task being to affirm monotheism. There is only one God – Yahweh is the God of the whole earth – without equal or rival. It's a call for loyalty that has direct and concrete moral implications for the Israelites. It was a call for them to live their lives under the Lordship of one God.

The problem was, even though Yahweh had commanded that he should be Israel's only God, in the Ancient Near East there was a pantheon of gods vying for attention – Asherah, Baal, Anath and Dagon, to name but a few.

In fact, as Joshua reminds the tribes of Israel, the worship of other gods was part of their history: 'Long ago your ancestors lived on the other side of the Euphrates River, and they worshipped other gods' (Joshua 24:2 CEV).

But if we read the story of the Old Testament carefully, we soon discover that Israel was frequently tempted to return to worshipping those 'other gods'. Which isn't surprising when you realise that, in their understanding – which had filtered into their worldview from the traditions of the cultures that surrounded them – everything depended on the favour of the gods. The gods decided such life-sustaining issues as the success of the annual harvest (which, in an agriculturally based society, was literally a matter of life or death), protection from natural disasters, victory in war, good health and so on.

Though these other gods were typically impersonal, angry, unpredictable and remote, and only accessible through complex and demanding ritual and sacrifice in designated holy places, they did claim to be all-powerful. So it still made sense that if they appeared to be doing a better job of protecting and prospering those who worshipped them than Yahweh was, then perhaps it might be time for Israel to make the smart move and switch allegiances.

Yahweh – often translated as 'LORD' (printed in capital and small-capital letters) in our contemporary Bibles – is the distinctive, personal name of the God of Israel.[2] In fact, Yahweh is the most frequently used name for God in the Old Testament, appearing over 6,800 times.

There are various theories about the deeper meaning of the name Yahweh (I Am). According to one tradition it means 'to be, to become'. Another regards it as meaning 'He was; He is; He will be'. But as Michael Goheen and Craig Bartholomew have noted, 'Perhaps the best translation of this expression is 'I will be who I Am'.[3]

Whatever the exact content of the name, calling yourself 'I Am', on first hearing, seems very strange; indeed, rather than a response to Moses' question, it's actually more of a non-response. A veiling rather than an unveiling. 'Who are you?' Moses asks. 'I Am' comes the response. That's it? 'You are what?' Moses could have retorted.

In reality, however, 'Yahweh' was not only the most intriguing but the most profound response that the God of Israel could have given to Moses' question, for it leaves the whole question of who he is and what he is like totally open. Yahweh refuses to be labelled, boxed or summed up in a word – instead, he will only come to be known as, and if, the people of Israel choose to journey with him. Yahweh is who Israel will discover him to be as their relationship with him develops.

We see some of the significance of all this if we consider the context in which 'I Am' reveals himself to the people of Israel.

The ancient Egyptian sun god, Aten, was worshipped as 'Creator of all ... Valiant Shepherd'. Amon-Re, another Egyptian god, was hailed as

> The lord of truth and father of the gods.
> Who made mankind and created the beasts.
> Lord of what is ... Who made what is below and
>   what is above ...
> The Sovereign.[4]

And Enlil, the Babylonian god, who Israel would encounter during their exile (586 B.C.), was

Judge and decision maker.

[Whose] word is ... life's breath ...

Enlil, you are the good shepherd.[5]

So, if the god of the burning bush had said to Moses, tell the people 'I Am the Creator of all', 'the great Shepherd', 'the Father' or 'the judge of all', then actually he could have been easily mistaken for an array of other Ancient Near Eastern gods. He could have then been perceived as having the same kind of character and morality that all these other gods were known for – despite their grand titles.

Instead, what Yahweh does is to make it clear to Moses and Israel – 'Don't confuse me with any other god. And don't try to box me in. At this stage you have no language for defining me. I Am different. So instead, let me surprise you. For I will be who I will be, and you will slowly discover just what this means in the unfolding relationship that develops between us.'

The very name *Yahweh* is an invitation to discover, an enticement to an adventure of slow revelation. Any other label at this stage would not only have been superficial, but even misleading. The god who speaks out of the burning bush is simply inferring, 'I'm different; journey with me; you will not regret it'. As Terrence Fretheim wrote, 'The name [Yahweh] will shape Israel's story, but the story will also give greater texture to the name.'[6]

It is Yahweh's differentness that is the foundation of Israel's story and their moral framework and formation. But who this Yahweh is will only be discovered in an ongoing, committed relationship with him. His distinctiveness will not be determined by preconceived or borrowed ideas about other gods – past, present or future.

Israel will come to know Yahweh as Creator, but as they do so they will discover that his morality and behaviour are in stark contrast to the gods of the other popular creation stories being told in the Ancient Near East. As Walter Brueggemann makes clear, in contrast to other gods who lay claim to creation, 'Yahweh's work ... is never an act of raw, sovereign power, but is an act saturated with covenantal, ethical intentionality.'[7]

The point is this: while the names and metaphors Israel will come to use for their God may not be unique, the character of their God was matchless.

More than that, the Israelites will discover that they have a central role in creation rather than being a mere afterthought of the gods (a very common idea in the Ancient Near East). They will slowly realise that they are called to live out a distinctive moral vision as Yahweh's ambassadors, modelling his justice, his mercy and his concern for the oppressed, the stranger, the widow and the orphan.

It is interesting that so much modern theology is preoccupied with the question of whether God exists. We assume that the first step in theology is to convince modern people that God is there. The Old Testament, however, and indeed the entire Bible, is concerned with a different and more important question: What kind of God exists?

Set in Story

Though our Bibles start in the obvious place, with the creation of the universe, in many ways the story of the God we worship – Yahweh, the God of Israel – begins later with a people enslaved by the Egyptian Pharaoh, and the promise that he will deliver them from their bondage and oppression. 'I have seen how my people are suffering as slaves in Egypt ... and I have come down to rescue them' (Exodus 3:7–8 CEV).

Of course, before the Exodus story comes the original calling of Abram (Genesis 12), which reveals God – and uses the name *Yahweh* – who, in contrast to other ancient gods, was close at hand, engaged with his world and discovered through personal encounter within the day-to-day realities of life. He was the faithful God who would bless Abram and make his countless descendants into a great nation.[8]

Making himself known, Yahweh promises Abram (and his descendants) a land of their own in which they will prosper: 'Leave your country, your family, and your relatives and go to the land that I will show you. I will bless you and make your descendents into a great nation.' And right from the start, God's goal is clearly that his generosity should be shared universally, adding that, 'everyone on earth will be blessed because of you' (Genesis 12:1–3 CEV).

Some scholars believe that from the standpoint of God's revelation of himself as 'I Am' to Moses, the authors of the Pentateuch (the first five books of the Bible, commonly known as the Books of Moses) then write their new understanding of their God as Yahweh back into the earlier story of the calling of Abram. After all, Exodus 6:2 (CEV) contains the clear statement by Yahweh that, 'My name is the LORD [Yahweh]. But when I appeared to Abraham, Isaac, and Jacob, I came as God All-Powerful [El Shaddai] and did not use my name,' which seems to contradict the account in Genesis.

Others believe that Yahweh originally revealed himself to Abram as just that. But because the Israelites had been enslaved in Egypt for four hundred years and were surrounded by many other gods, Moses needed to be reminded that the god speaking to him, and claiming to be concerned for his people, from a burning bush, is none other than Yahweh – who, as the God of the whole earth (including Egypt), is not territorially bound.

Whatever the truth, the story of the Exodus becomes one of the most important, foundational, God-revealing, people-shaping moments of the Old Testament. It serves as an axis on which so much of the whole story of Israel turns. As the Old Testament professor Walter Brueggemann writes, 'Israel characteristically retold all of its experience through the powerful, definitional lens of the of the Exodus memory.'[9]

Exodus is like a pair of spectacles through which Israel learned to understand the whole of their story. It is as though the people of Israel only really begin to make sense of themselves, their story, and who God [Yahweh] is from this vantage point. As author John Drane says,

> When later generations wanted to remind themselves of the character of their God, they turned to the exodus story. This event was celebrated in poetry and in song, and reported in family groups at every opportunity. It became the central focus of their faith. Not only did it remind them that God was active in history: it also gave a unique insight into the nature of that activity – and therefore into the character of God himself.[10]

'Thou Shalt Not!'

For many people, the God of the Bible is simply a lawgiver, a rule writer, a despot who commands and demands of his human subjects that they follow the letter of his dictates unswervingly – even unthinkingly. But is that really the way we are supposed to understand the moral vision set out by Yahweh in Scripture?

It is often forgotten that the Ten Commandments are given in Exodus chapter 20[11] and not in Exodus chapter 1. In other words, they emerge within the context of a story and a relationship. Therefore, any attempt to pluck these ten sentences (or the rest of Law that follows them) out of the biblical text – and their context – in a disembodied way and then use them as a rulebook for life, is a huge misjudgement. It is impossible to understand the Law without first understanding Israel's story of liberation.

We do well to listen to Old Testament scholar Andrew Sloane, who warns, 'It is possible to take [the Old Testament Law] out of its canonical context and look at it as an isolated, abstract set of religious and moral commands (and many books on ethics do exactly that), but to do so would be a mistake.'[12]

Actually, any *'biblical'* teaching that ignores the cultural context of the text is likely to diminish rather than enhance the authority of Scripture, however loud and dogmatic the claims it makes for itself.

The Ten Commandments are not random rules. Though God descends on a mountain to give them (and the rest of the Law) to the newly formed community of Israel, these regulations have not simply 'dropped out of the sky'. Rather, the Law that Moses receives is a dimension – a partial expression – of the moral vision that is becoming ever clearer from the relationship that Yahweh is building with Israel and the journey that they are on together.

It is easy to make the mistake of thinking that biblical ethics are set in stone, when in fact, they are set within a story – and it is that story that makes all the difference.

So, in introducing Moses to the Ten Commandments, Yahweh tells a story: I Am none other than the God who 'brought you out of Egypt, out of the land of slavery' (Exodus 20:2). Knowing, understanding and living in that story is key to making sense of what follows.

These commands are not an account of how life has to be lived just because Yahweh says so. They are an expression of how life ought to be lived, given who Yahweh is revealing himself to be: 'I Am: the God who is compassionate, merciful, loving, caring, patient. This is how you can be like me and live the same way.'

A few years ago, I was taking part in a live debate on *BBC Radio 5 Live*. As we chatted, the presenter chipped in with an observation not untypical of the sort of thing many of us have probably had thrown at our feet: 'Why is God so miserable? Why has he got such a downer on everything we do? Don't do this and don't do that. Don't desire what other people have got. Don't lie. Don't commit adultery. It's pathetic.'

I interrupted her with a question. 'Does it really say those things, I mean, does God really say, "Don't commit adultery"?'

'Yes he does,' came her rapier reply.

'Well, I've never read that bit,' I said.

'You know very well it's in the Bible,' she retorted. 'It's one of the Ten Commandments.'

'Oh, now I know what you're talking about,' I exclaimed. 'It's just that I didn't recognise it at first because of the tone of voice you were using.'

'What do you mean?'

'You're absolutely right,' I continued. 'God does say that we shouldn't commit adultery, but not in the way you've read it. You see, before he gives any of the Ten Commandments he introduces himself as the God who loves Israel. He lets them know that he is for them, not against them. He wants the best for them. God didn't sit in heaven making a list of all the things he knows human beings like to do and then outlaw them all to spoil our fun. God didn't start his relationship with human beings by drawing up a list of moral rules that they had to keep. They are God saying, "I love you. I'm on your side. I got you out of slavery. I'm the best deal you've got going for you. Trust me. Don't steal. Don't lie. Don't abandon me. Don't commit adultery, because if you do it will unleash destructive powers that will slowly overshadow you, destroying you, your families and your society".'

The presenter looked at me in astonishment. 'No one has ever explained it to me in that way,' she said quietly. 'That makes so much sense.'

When we look more deeply, we are enabled to see that the commandments' 'primary function is to shape a moral vision, to give us a picture of the character of God and God's people, rather than to give us a list of rules to live by',[13] says Andrew Sloane. They speak of attitudes and virtues that both underpin and go beyond themselves. Yes, what they command matters. But what they represent matters far more.

More than this, the Ten Commandments are clearly not an exhaustive list of rules and regulations that will guide Israel through every ethical decision they will face; a fact that the Jews themselves understood from the start.

In fact, Jewish tradition holds that the written Law did not stand alone but was handed down with an accompanying oral tradition – known as the *Mishnah*. This oral tradition expanded on the text and provided commentary on what it meant and how to live it. It provided a guide to interpretation of the authoritative written Law, with explanations of the Torah's meaning and application to everyday life.[14] As John Rogerson, Professor of Biblical Studies at Sheffield University, puts it:

> Because the laws actually contained in the scriptures deal with only very limited areas of life, Jews believe that God revealed two laws to Moses on Mt Sinai – a written law and an oral law. The former is found in the Jewish scriptures, and pre-eminently in the first five books (the Torah). The second was passed down by word of mouth from Moses to Joshua to the prophets, and eventually to the rabbis ... who began to write it down in the Mishnah (early 3rd century C.E. [A.D.]) ... there has been, and continues to be, a process of legal and scriptural interpretation within Judaism designed to discover God's will for every detail of life.[15]

More than Meets the Eye

The journey that Yahweh was taking Israel on was multifaceted. It was physical. He was carrying them out of slavery in Egypt, across a lifeless desert to a land flowing with milk and honey. But it was also a moral journey. Paganism – the stories of the many other gods of the Ancient Near East – was the air the people of Israel had breathed in from the cultures that surrounded them, and to some extent, it had captured their thinking and subverted their moral responses. (See the episode of the golden calf in Exodus 32, for example.)

Yahweh was leading the people of Israel away from these misshapen and distorted ideas about the divine, themselves, their role in the world and their ethical responses to others, and slowly introducing them to himself and a different way of living and being human.

Without the backdrop of this big picture, some of the individual verses of the Law (the code for life set out in the Pentateuch) can – and indeed often do – sound alarming to our ears. Even amongst those who make the claim that they teach the whole Bible as literal and timeless truth, the 'let's find a proof text and live by it' approach to moral choices simply doesn't work.

In an insightful scene from the TV series *The West Wing*, the fictional American president, Jed Bartlet (Martin Sheen), arrives back at the White House to host a reception for a small group of broadcasters. Among the group is a woman by the name of Dr Jacobs.

The president begins to address the group, but he finds himself constantly distracted by Dr Jacobs' presence. Eventually he turns to her and asks, 'I'm sorry. You're Dr Jacobs?'

'Right?' She nods.

'It's good to have you here,' says Bartlet.

Having established that his visitor is who he thinks she is, the president carries on addressing his guests for another sentence or two. But then, once again, he becomes distracted by her. 'Forgive me, Dr Jacobs, are you an MD?' he asks.

'A PhD,' she answers.

'A PhD?'

'Yes, sir.'

'Psychology?' enquires the president.

'No, sir.'

'Theology?'

'No.'

'Social work?'

Finally, in a frustrated tone, Dr Jacobs answers, 'I have a PhD in English literature.'

'I'm asking because on your show people call in for advice, and you go by the name Dr Jacobs, and I don't know if maybe your listeners were confused by that and assumed you had advanced training in theology, psychology or health care.'

'I don't believe they are confused. No, sir.'

'Good. I like your show ... I like how you call homosexuality an abomination.'

'I don't say homosexuality is an abomination Mr President. The Bible does.'

'Yes, it does. Leviticus – '

'18:22!' Dr. Jacobs quickly exclaims.

'Chapter and verse,' replies the president, before continuing. 'I want to ask you a couple of questions while I have you here.... I'm interested in selling my youngest daughter into slavery, as sanctioned in Exodus 21:7. She's a Georgetown sophomore, speaks fluent Italian, always cleared the table when it was her turn. What would be a good price for her?

'While you are thinking about that can I ask another? My Chief of Staff, Leo McGarry, insists on working on the Sabbath. Exodus 35:2 clearly says he should be put to death. Am I morally obligated to kill him myself, or is it okay to call the police?

'Here's one that's really important, 'cause we've got a lot of sports fans in this town. Touching the skin of a dead pig makes one unclean.

Leviticus 11:7–8. If they promise to wear gloves, can the Washington Redskins still play football?

'Does the whole town really have to be together to stone my brother John for planting different crops side by side?

'Can I burn my mother in a small family gathering for wearing garments made from two different threads?

'Think about those questions, would you?'[16]

As this exchange between President Bartlet and Dr Jacobs proves, when detached from their narrative context, the rules and regulations of the Law become a rigid, inflexible way of understanding Scripture, doing ethics and trying to determine how to live. In fact, they can become ridiculous or even abusive. And yet many Christians are still under the impression that the narrative of Scripture – which takes seriously the setting, culture and context of the story of the Bible – is unimportant.

We want 'pure' truth that can be quarried from the text for all time, without the burden of dealing with the circumstances of the story – which is probably one reason why we latch onto rules, regulations and commands so readily.

We have become convinced that adults should be able to deal in pure, unadulterated facts. Stories are for kids. And so the stories of Israel – and indeed of Jesus – are, for the most part, relegated to the Sunday school curriculum and action songs. Grown-ups can deal with solid doctrine – teaching on 'sanctification', 'holiness' and 'justification' – real meat!

Formulaic and propositional terms and statements alone, however, provide a poor understanding of the complexities of God's action and interaction with the world. Story is essential. To miss this is to miss the heart of the way that God has always chosen to interact with his people.

We throw around theological and doctrinal ideas about God as 'creator', or 'judge', or 'almighty', but what do these concepts actually mean? They are nothing more than a convenient shorthand for use by those who are already soaked in the story. But for those who don't know it, or don't know it well enough, they are empty and meaningless, or worse still, confusing and misleading. As theologians Stanley Hauerwas and William H. Willimon argue:

> Our contention is that it does not just happen that God's people tell stories; certainly, the penchant for storytelling has nothing to do with [these people] being primitive, pre-rational ... whereas we are sophisticated people who do not. Story is the fundamental means of talking about and listening to God, the only human means available to us that is complex and engaging enough to make comprehensible what it means to be with God.[17]

So it is that before God even delivers the first of the Ten Commandments, he reminds Moses, subsequent generations of the children of Israel – and twenty-first century Christians – of the story and context that underpins them.

Telling the Story

> 'Listen, Israel! The LORD our God is the only true God! So love the LORD your God with all your heart, soul, and strength. Memorise his laws and tell them to your children, over and over again. Talk about them all the time, whether you're at home or walking along the road or going to bed at night, or getting up in the morning. Write down copies and tie them to your wrists and foreheads to help you obey them. Write these laws on the door frames of your homes and on your town gates.
> 'The LORD promised your ancestors Abraham, Isaac, and Jacob that he would give you this land ... don't forget it was

*the LORD who set you free from slavery and brought you out
of Egypt ...
We were slaves of the king of Egypt, but the LORD used
his great power and set us free. We saw him perform miracles
and make horrible things happen to the king, his officials, and
everyone else.' (Deuteronomy 6:4–22 CEV)*

Israel understood how important it was to gather to tell and retell
their story to each other and to their children. In this way, their values
were constantly reiterated and passed on to new generations. That's
why they put so much emphasis on acts of corporate worship and
meditation. Indeed, in centuries still to come, in exile in Babylon or
trapped in the ghettos of central Europe, these habits and traditions
would become even more vital to their survival.

And every Jew knew that it was their responsibility not just to tell this
story to their young, but to live it out before them, in their attitudes,
habits, behaviour and daily moral choices. If this did not happen, the
world would become very confusing and the story mistrusted. More
than that, without a clear and truthful account of the world and your
destiny, it becomes impossible to make sense of life and how to live.

You can almost imagine a Jewish father in exile telling his children:
'Such behaviour is fine for them, but not for us. We are special. We
are different. We have a different story. We have a different set of
values. We are part of Israel.'

It is one thing to know the commands – 'Do not kill', 'Do not commit adultery', 'Do not bear false witness' – but where do we get the
strength from to overpower our baser instincts? Only a different
story – a different set of values, practices and relationships – can
empower us to live differently.

The power and potency of Israel's story is demonstrated particularly
vividly when we stop to ponder what an amazing act of courage and

faith it was for them, in the face of constant persecution through the ages, to go on having children and believing in tomorrow.

The story of Israel is fundamentally one of a people whose very existence – past, present and future – was about a journey with God. The Scriptures they read were simply an account of the adventure they were part of.

By attaching themselves to God's story and purpose, the everyday lives of the children of Israel were filled with deeper purpose and direction. They were part of the great adventure of discovering what God was doing and joining in to be part of it.

So it is, as the people told the story of Moses being given the Law, they never understood it as an arbitrary set of commands, but rather a counter-story against that of the oppressive culture of Egypt, its Pharaoh, and the misery they had lived under for so long.

That is the key – not to read the Law with blinkers on – but to ask what it tells us about Yahweh in the context of the unravelling story of Israel. For it was in telling this story that the children of Israel came to understand themselves as a people on a journey, a people on a huge adventure, with a Law that contained the morality necessary to sustain them on the road.

imaginative

As a young boy I used to attend Sunday school at my local church. On one particular Sunday, the teacher decided that he wanted to demonstrate why it was that, in the famous Old Testament story, even though Moses was allowed to see God pass by, glimpsing something of his glory, he was told that he could not look upon God's face and live (Exodus 33).

Taking a piece of tissue paper, our teacher moved it slowly closer to the naked flame of a candle. But even before the tissue paper touched the flame, it burst into a ball of fire. 'God is like that', he triumphantly proclaimed to our amazed stares (once he'd extinguished the fire). 'God is holy. He is an all-consuming fire, and we are sinful. Which means that no one can get close to him without suffering the same fate as this piece of paper did when it got too close to the candle's flame.'

This vivid illustration stuck in my mind, and for years it provided me with the basis of my understanding of what it meant for God to be holy. But the older I get, and with every rereading of the Bible, the more convinced I am that my teacher missed the point.

Get Holy

One of the central themes that runs throughout the story of God and the people of Israel, as they journey from slavery to liberation, is Yahweh's constant refrain: 'Be holy, because I am holy' (Leviticus 11:45; 19:2, etc.).

It is a well-known statement, but what exactly does it mean to say that God is holy?

And what does it mean for those who follow God to be holy?

It is true to say that the Christian Church has sometimes struggled when it comes to understanding and interpreting holiness. Though we sing a lot about the fact that God is holy, and our desire is to be the same, the question remains, what would it look like if we were?

Typically, holiness has been defined by ideas of separation, isolation and withdrawal from the world. Over the centuries this has lead to the development of some strange notions that, besides anything else, have provided ideal comedy material.

In the second series of the classic British comedy *Blackadder*, the central character, Edmund Blackadder (played by Rowan Atkinson), challenges his friend Lord Melchett to a rowdy drinking competition at his house. The only problem is Edmund's aunt and uncle, Lord and Lady Whiteadder, two of the most fanatical puritans in England, have invited themselves over for dinner to discuss his inheritance.

'Aunt. Uncle. How lovely to see you,' says Edmund.

'Wicked child! Don't lie,' exclaims Edmund's aunt, slapping him across his face. 'Everyone hates us and you know it.'

Taken aback, Edmund shows his relatives into the dining room. 'If you'd like to help yourself to a chair.'

'A chair! You have chairs in your house? Wicked child. Chairs are an invention of Satan. In our house Nathanial sits on a spike.'

'And yourself?' enquires Blackadder.

'I sit on Nathanial,' explains Aunt Whiteadder. 'Two spikes would be an extravagance. I will suffer comfort this once. We will just have to stick forks in our legs between courses. I trust you remember we eat no meat.'

'Heaven forbid. No, here we feast only on God's lovely turnip – mashed,' says Edmund, assuming that for once he has the measure of his puritanical aunt and uncle.

'Mashed! Mashing is also the work of Beelzebub. For Satan saw God's blessed turnip and he envied it and he mashed it to spoil its sacred shape.'

'Now Aunty,' begins Edmund, trying to move the conversation on to the matter of his inheritance – but to no avail.

'Don't call me Aunty. Aunty is a relative and relatives are evidence of sex. And sex is hardly a fitting conversation for the dinner table.'[18]

And so the ridiculous conversation continues.

Of course, this is comedic exaggeration. But good comedy works because it is painfully never far from the truth.

In the pursuit of holiness, sections of the Church – ones that, over the years, I have personally encountered – have banned dancing, disapproved or even prohibited the frequenting of the cinema, labelled pop music as a tool of the Devil, banned alcohol and insisted that women have their heads covered for worship and remain silent.

In my childhood I was part of a church with a strict dress code that somehow, in my psyche, became linked to the concept of holiness. Everyone knew what was acceptable and what was not. For women, makeup and jewellery were out, as were trousers. Hats, however, were obligatory and sensible shoes were preferable. For men, essential Sunday wear consisted of a suit (or failing that, at least a pair of smart 'pressed' trousers), worn with a shirt and tie. Denim and T-shirts were definitely a no-go for either sex!

I remember the time I led a Communion service in the church where I first worked as a minister, without wearing a tie. One of the senior leaders wrote to me the very next day asking for my resignation.

Over the last few decades – and under the guise of the quest for holiness – countless battles have also been fought over which musical instruments are worthy of being used to worship God. For some, only the church organ was ever up to the job (and preferably not one of those modern electronic things either!). Drums and guitars (especially electric ones) are, on the other hand, 'the tools of Satan'. In truth, this situation is particularly ironic because it lacks any historical perspective.

When organs first began to enter popular use in ordinary church buildings, there was great outcry against them because they were widely used in the music halls of the time (which had a reputation for drunkenness and debauchery). And in some church traditions this angst was doubly as deep because, until then, any musical instrument was regarded as a vain distraction from holy meditation, and all hymns were therefore sung or chanted unaccompanied.

Perhaps one of the most bizarre prohibitions was a church-led campaign against the introduction of the zip fastener in the early years of the twentieth century, after its invention in America in 1914 by Gideon Sundbäck. It was widely believed to be morally dubious on the grounds that it was quick and easy to undo and, therefore, sexually suggestive! And partly because of this, it wasn't until 1937 that the zipper finally beat the button for usage in trousers.

In the late 1980s and early 1990s (before my hair went grey), I would often be asked to speak at larger, even international, youth events. Typically, the instruction given to me by the organisers would be to do something 'evangelistic' or 'about missions' or 'on holiness'. Holiness, in this setting, was code for warning teenagers about the dangers of premarital sex and the consumption, at any time, of alcohol. Holiness was exclusively linked to personal piety.

And if you look back through Church history, you find that asceticism has often been offered as the key to holiness, insisting that if you simply retreat into your own world, you will experience more of God. A famous example is the fifth-century monk Saint Simeon Stylites, who spent years living on a platform at the top of a pole. He lived in complete isolation, believing that such remoteness would help him to find the key to holiness. But sitting there, Mr Stylites discovered that his greatest problem was at the top of the pole – himself – rather than the world at the bottom!

I took a friend to have lunch in the café housed in our church building in central London. He had grown up in a denomination that described itself as part of the 'holiness movement'. As we enjoyed our soup, he suddenly realised that he was eating in what he referred to as, 'the sanctuary'. For him this was a huge moral problem. The 'sanctuary' is supposed to be 'set aside' for 'higher things' he exclaimed. Though he didn't leave, it was obvious that he felt extremely uncomfortable. Holiness for him was about a 'special' place and 'special' activities.

Looking Deeper

So the question must be posed: What is holiness – and is it all really this negative?

'The meaning of "holy/holiness",' as Gerald Hawthorne has noted, 'is not exhausted with such ideas as "separate from", "dedicated to", "sacred" and the like.... There are also ethical and moral meanings attached to them.'[19]

The fact is, the concept of holiness is not about 'absence' but very much about 'distinctive presence'. It is not about withdrawal but engagement. It is not just about what we term the 'spiritual' but especially about the ordinary. Holiness is about a particular ethical presence within the world, never a withdrawal from it.

The word *holy* originally literally meant 'different' or 'other'. Since then, however, it has become encrusted with layer after layer of cultural misinterpretation, and the direction of travel has not been good. The problem is that the idea of holiness as 'differentness', in the sense of 'distinctiveness', was soon, and in some ways quite naturally, expressed as 'separateness'. But from there, it was all too easy to slide into an unhelpful and misleading mind-set dominated by thoughts of 'withdrawal', 'detachment' and 'isolation', which gradually distorted, obscured and even obliterated the real meaning of the word.

These negative views were fed, however, not by Hebrew and biblical thought, but by other influences. As soon as Christianity spread beyond its Jewish origins in the first century, it began to encounter Hellenistic (Greek) culture, which had been profoundly shaped and influenced by the thought and teaching of the philosopher Plato. Plato (c. 427–348 B.C.) helped to lay the foundations of Western philosophy and was also the founder of the Academy in Athens, the first institution of higher learning in the Western world.

Where the Hebrew tradition sought to hold what we would call the 'physical' and the 'spiritual' and see them as a unity (indeed, Hebrew has no language to do otherwise, for all of life is God's stage), Plato wanted to separate them. As far as he was concerned, what is good is 'spiritual' (invisible and immortal), while all that is bad is 'physical'. He taught that each human person consists of a physical body and an invisible soul. The body is transient and ultimately worthless. The soul (the divine spark), however, is immortal – it came from the invisible spiritual world and, having been freed from the prison of its physical moorings at death, will return to it.

The influence of this kind of thought on the Church was enormous. It encouraged an understanding of 'spirituality' that was essentially world-denying. God was utterly transcendent – not only beyond the trivia of daily life and the petty concerns of the physical world, but unaffected by them. Holiness was, therefore, all about withdrawal and separation.

Doing Life Differently

When the first Hebrews heard Yahweh's challenge to them to 'be holy as I am holy', they simply heard, 'Be different as I am different.' So the real questions are, What is God's difference and how can we copy it?

You can't define holiness without having a context in which to do so. Holiness only makes sense when set against, or held up to, something else. And as we have seen, Yahweh's holiness, or differentness, was seen in relation to the difference of his character to those of the many other gods of the Ancient Near East region who were famous for their unfeeling, irrational, angry and capricious natures.

As John Drane points out,

> Many religious people think of their gods only in terms of awe-inspiring power. But Israel's covenant faith led to a distinctive understanding of what it means to be holy ... the events of Israel's history had shown that the God of the Old Testament was faithful and trustworthy.... God's holiness was a way of behaving.[20]

That is Yahweh's difference. That is his holiness.

In the words of the prophet Isaiah: 'Our holy God lives forever in the highest heavens, and this is what he says: 'Though I live high above in the holy place, I am here to help those who are humble and depend only on me' (Isaiah 57:15 CEV).

With Yahweh, holiness is not about an otherness that is removed and isolated from this world, but exactly the opposite; he is involved with his people and on their side. It is this that sets Yahweh apart from other gods.

In fact, holiness, or 'differentness', is an umbrella term – the short-hand way of summing up the whole of Yahweh's character, or nature. And this, of course, had massive implications for ancient Israel – just as it does for the Church today.

So, if we are to be morally different in the same way that Yahweh is morally different, his kind of holiness must form the basis for our moral vision and responses. And for the Church, just as Israel's call to holiness was a commission to demonstrate a way of life that was distinctive from that on display in other communities and nations, so ours is to live distinctively in the same way. As Gerald Hawthorne states:

> God the Holy One took the initiative to reveal himself to Israel at Sinai and to call this people out from among other nations into a special personal relationship with himself. Thus, it was God who made Israel a holy nation (Exodus 19:6; Deuteronomy 7:6), a people that must preserve its distinctiveness by pursuing a way of life different from that practiced by other peoples. (Deuteronomy 7:5–6)[21]

This also explains why so many of the individual moral instructions found in the Old Testament have the prefix 'I am the LORD your God, I am Holy and you must be holy too!'

'Be Holy as I am holy' – God's constant refrain – is his repeated invitation to his people to imitate him, to participate in his character, and the rest of the Pentateuch is the detailed, contextual outworking of that.

Take, for instance, this selection of instructions in Leviticus 19:

> *I am the LORD your God. I am holy, and you must be holy too! Respect your father and your mother. . . . When you harvest your grain, always leave some of it standing along the edges of your fields and don't pick up what falls on the ground. Don't strip your grapevines. . . . Leave them for the poor and for those foreigners who live among you. . . . Do not steal or tell lies or cheat*

others ... Don't fail to pay your workers.... Be fair, no matter
who is on trial – don't favour either the poor or the rich.... Stop
being angry and don't try to take revenge.... Love others as
much as you love yourself.... respect ... older people.... Don't
mistreat any foreigners who live in your land.... Use honest
scales. (Leviticus 19:1–36 CEV)

The theme of the text is straightforward. It is simply about Israel's responsibility to reflect Yahweh in their everyday relationships, dealings and decisions. And their story was filled with a rich depth in its description of Yahweh's character as discovered on their journey with him.

To take just two of a myriad of examples:

Exodus 34:6 explains that Yahweh is 'the compassionate and gracious God, slow to anger, abounding in love and faithfulness' and Deuteronomy 32:4 that 'he is the Rock, his works are perfect, and all his ways are just. A faithful God who does no wrong, upright and just is he.' Just these two texts speak of Yahweh's compassion, graciousness, mercy, patience, faithfulness, justice, wisdom, reliability, trustworthiness and consistency.

As the penny drops and Yahweh's distinctive way of being is adopted by Israel, then they too will become 'holy'. Their way of life – of being human – is to be as distinct from the ethical, political, religious and social practices of their Ancient Near East neighbours, as Yahweh's character is from those of the gods whom they worship.

Holiness, it turns out, is about developing the right habits and learning to live beautifully, which is one reason why, for example, Sabbath was so important to the moral vision in Israel. 'Remember the Sabbath day by keeping it holy' (Exodus 20:8).

To keep the Sabbath – to allow for re-creational and celebration time – was a principle in direct contrast with the world of Pharaoh, in which no rest was given to the people of Israel, and no mercy shown to those who had become exhausted, or were unable to work because of sickness, injury or disability.[22]

Therefore, once they were liberated from such oppression by Yahweh, it was vital that the community of Israel took a stand against those 'unholy' or 'un-Yahweh-like' practices.

'It's as if God says, "You've experienced Egypt; now I'm calling you to be the anti-Egypt,"' writes Rob Bell.[23]

But if Israel were to fully express God's holiness, then keeping the Sabbath holy could not be allowed to descend into a legalistic setting-aside of one day each week for inactivity. Which is something we come to understand later, when Jesus encounters the hostility of the Jewish leaders of his day over the unorthodox way he chooses to conduct himself on the Sabbath.

> *[Jesus] went into their synagogue, and a man with a shrivelled hand was there. Looking for a reason to accuse Jesus, they asked him, 'Is it lawful to heal on the Sabbath?' He said to them, 'If any of you has a sheep and it falls into a pit on the Sabbath, will you not take hold of it and lift it out? How much more valuable is a man than a sheep! Therefore it is lawful to do good on the Sabbath.' (Matthew 12:9–12)[24]*

The point Jesus is making is this: you can't claim to be keeping the Sabbath holy and then use what was designed to bring liberation to ordinary people as a new tool for oppression and lack of compassion. God's character is generous, compassionate, merciful, faithful and just. To bring healing is to keep the Sabbath holy simply because it is part and parcel of an authentic expression and celebration of God's character, out of which the Law and the moral vision of Israel both flow.

Stephen Westerholm observes,

> When opposed [Jesus] does not reply by arguing that, counter to his opponents' claims, 'work' has not been done nor

the command transgressed. He insists that doing 'good' can never be wrong on the Sabbath, that compassion is a better guide to proper behaviour than rules defined by legal experts (Matthew 12:10–11), that God's intentions for the Sabbath are distorted when humans are subjected to rigid code.[25]

As Jesus himself said just prior to this incident – 'I desire mercy, not sacrifice' (Matthew 12:7).

Virtue Vision

Through the centuries humanity has wrestled with the question of the best way to determine right from wrong and make wise moral choices. Though many theories have been developed, they all basically fit into one of three core approaches – Rules, Consequences or Virtues.[26]

The 'rule book', or 'obligation', theories are technically known as 'deontological ethics' (from Greek *deon*, meaning 'obligation or duty'). They place their emphasis on obedience to moral absolutes and hold that, in the light of these, any behaviour can be seen as inherently good or evil, regardless of its consequences. So, for instance, we have a duty to do those things that are inherently good (like 'truth-telling') regardless of the outcome.

Likewise, if God has commanded people not to work on the Sabbath, then people act rightly if they do not work on the Sabbath, simply because God has commanded that they do not do so.

In practice, however, not only is this sometimes impractical, insensitive and simplistic, it can even become immoral. For example, do we have a moral duty to always tell the truth, even to a known murderer who asks us where their next intended victim is?

And what if a friend's house is burning down on the Sabbath and I am a fireman? Can I help put the fire out, or is that breaking God's Law? And is it wrong for the fire station to be manned on a Sabbath?

Another huge problem with a rulebook approach is that you have to keep inventing new rules for unforeseen or nuanced situations. And the more you have, the more like a badly fitting, inflexible, unbending and suffocating straightjacket it becomes.

And then there is the problem of which rule should take priority when the rules that undergird your ethical system seem to clash – for example, the principle of truth with that of love in the question: Should I lie to protect a friend?

Many people desperately want a single right answer to each and every ethical question because they find moral ambiguity so hard to live with. They genuinely want to do the 'right thing', and even if they can't work out what that 'right thing' is, they like the idea that 'somewhere 'there is one right answer. But the problem is that, in reality, life is just far more complex than that.

If the Bible's revelation of Yahweh is central to our moral vision, that vision is not of an ethic based exhaustively, nor even primarily, on the kind of inflexible 'rulebook' approach that the Church has so often fallen into the trap of supporting and proclaiming. The Bible is first and foremost a story-based moral vision rather than a list of universal rules. Believing that the whole of life is somehow covered by the Ten Commandments and the Old Testament Law is even more unrealistic than it is optimistic.

In reaction to all this, an alternative approach, technically known as 'teleological ethics' (from the Greek *telos*, meaning 'end') developed. This way of thinking is popularly known as 'consequentialism' or 'utilitarianism'. Here the morality of any action is determined not by whether the rules were kept, but by its consequences. The ends justify the means. Of any two actions, the most ethical one will produce the greatest balance of benefits over harms.

Instead of saying that humans have a moral duty to abstain from murder, a consequentialist would say that we should abstain from murder because it has a number of undesirable effects. But then, just to stir things up, one might point, for instance, to the occasion when the famous pacifist, church leader and theologian Dietrich Bonhoeffer took part in a plot to assassinate Hitler, and ask whether that was good or bad.

So, for example, is warfare, and all the accompanying harm done through death, injuries and destruction of all parties involved, balanced by the good achieved in ending terrorism?

Once again, in practice there are some serious problems with this kind of approach. For instance, who decides what sort of consequences count as good or bad? How are those consequences measured objectively? And who does the judging?

Both the rules and consequences approaches to making ethical decisions are flawed, not only because they are too simplistic to cope with the complexity of life, but, as we shall discover, they fail to deal with the real issue at the heart of every moral choice: the moral formation and character of the people involved in making it.

What we see developed through the biblical story is much more in line with the ancient approach to morality, which today is known as 'virtue ethics'. Instead of relying on rules or trying to pre-guess consequences, this approach emphasises the person or community involved in the decision making and concentrates on the development of their moral character as the key element in the ethical choices they make and the way that they choose to live.

The development of character traits or habits, such as honesty, justice and integrity, enable us to act wisely and in line with our beliefs. Therefore, the question we should ask of any action is, What kind of person will I become if I do this?

Virtue (or character) ethics places an emphasis on being rather than doing, not because doing is nonessential, but because our actions are (even allowing for our fallen human nature and our mistakes) to a great extent a reflection of who we are.

The problem is, however, if morality hinges on the development of some intrinsic virtues, how do we know which ones they should be? And how do we define them? For instance, not everybody's idea of love is the same, or even anything near it.

It is only in the light of the story of Yahweh and his people that we discover an adequate basis to answer these questions. Who we are – and, therefore, how we behave – has everything to do with the story we choose to put our faith in. Stories, as they say, have the power to form whole worlds.

Only in the light of God's challenge to us to be holy – as he is – are we given the essential reference point that we need to see things with different eyes and develop a way of living – a morality – that works because it reflects him. In the light of his character, not only can we begin to define the content of love or justice, we are also equipped to answer the essential questions, Who am I? Who do I want to become? and How do I want to behave? As Stanley Hauerwas puts it, 'Ethics is first a way of seeing before it is a matter of doing.'[27]

The rapid emergence of abolitionist thinking in the slave-holding societies of the eighteenth-century Atlantic world is an example of this sort of 'seeing differently'. In Britain, France and British America, slave-holding, which had previously been thought to be morally neutral, or even virtuous, rapidly became viewed as evil among vast swathes of society and was eventually outlawed. While the emergence of abolitionist thought derived from a number of sources, central to its development was the work of William Wilberforce and the group of Christian friends, later to become known as the Clapham Sect.

Tragically, over the years that Wilberforce fought for the abolition of the slave trade, he found himself condemned by many Christians of his day. For instance, the bells of all Bristol's churches – a city built on the proceeds of the slave trade – were pealed merrily on the orders of the bishop, at the news of Parliament's rejection of Wilberforce's original bill for the abolition of the slave trade.[28]

Wilberforce was considered liberal and unbiblical because of his clear 'abandonment of the authority of Scripture'. In fact, on the basis of a straightforward reading of the text of both the Old and New Testaments, his critics were right.[29] Wilberforce and friends, however, believed that, rather than listening to isolated proof texts, their stance was based on the deeper resonance of the whole story of Scripture and the clarity of the direction of its moral journey. In other words, they believed that they could see things with different eyes.

Drip, Drip, Drip …

If all of this is true, then there is a burning question that must be faced: If God is so virtuous and we are to model the way we live on his character and the story of his life with his people, then why does the Old Testament contain so much material that depicts Yahweh as anything *but* virtuous? Why is he so often presented as angry, fierce, wrathful, cursing, violent, vengeful, sometimes genocidal and supportive of a justice system weighted towards males?

God's relationship with Israel took place in the messy and often brutal reality of their day-to-day lives, longings and ambitions. And in the Ancient Near East, where war and unrestrained violence were commonplace, having a god of power on your side helped justify cruel acts of revenge towards those who had wronged you.

More than that, the very fact that Israel claimed Yahweh is the one true God implied, according to their worldview, that he must be the most powerful god of all. So, when Israel went to war against her enemies, the expectation was that their god, the Lord Almighty, would demonstrate his power, destroy the opposing armies and in doing so vindicate his own name as well as Israel's belief in him.

41

That is why, if we focus in on individual Old Testament verses and stories, it's so easy to fall into the trap of seeing God as a vengeful despot. It's only when we allow ourselves to step back, to see the entire sweep of Israel's relationship with Yahweh and take in the bigger picture, that his desire to be a catalyst for change becomes clear. Only then can we grasp his struggle to communicate his love, not just for Israel, but for the whole human race, which was to eventually culminate in the arrival of Jesus.

Yahweh's association with the vengeance and violence of the Old Testament era wasn't a true expression of who he was so much as the result of his determination to be involved with his people. This unwillingness to distance himself from the people of Israel and their actions meant that at times he seems to be implicated in their excessive acts of violence. From the very beginning, Yahweh's dealings with Israel were motivated by his desire to demonstrate his love. But for a people saturated in a worldview dominated by gods of power and violence, it was inevitably going to be a slow uphill struggle to understand his true character and nature.

So, for instance, when placed against this cultural backdrop, the well-known and frequently quoted saying 'An eye for an eye', so often used, even today, to justify retaliation, actually becomes a unique ethic of constraint put in place to limit, rather than justify excessive violence and vengeful punishment and bring a sense of justice (see Exodus 21:24 and Leviticus 24:20–22).

Rather than legislating a mandatory sentence, it was there to set a maximum penalty beyond which it was unjust to go. According to the Old Testament ethicist Chris Wright, 'Possibly no other Old Testament text has been the victim of more misunderstanding and exaggeration than this one. Contrary to the popular view [God] does not condone rampant physical vengeance.... [This misconception] totally ignores the ethos of compassion, generosity, concern for the weak and restraint of the powerful that pervades [the Old Testament].'[30]

section two | imaginative

As you study the Old Testament, you can't help but sense the drip, drip of the slowly growing realisation that Yahweh is very different from the other gods. The truth is, the Bible never defines God as anger, power or judgement. As Karl Barth has pointed out, these attributes are never more than 'repetitions and amplifications of the one statement that God loves'.[31] If we forget this – if we ever talk about judgement or power outside of the context of God's love – we make a great mistake.

Even the stubborn children of Israel, with all their preconceived prejudices and cultural blinkers, slowly begin to see that, as the psalmists often had cause to write, 'The LORD ... is kind and patient, and his love never fails.... he doesn't punish us as our sins deserve' (Psalm 103:8, 10 CEV).[32]

thinking christianly

*I saw heaven standing open and there before me was a white
horse, whose rider is called Faithful and True. With justice
he judges and makes war.*

REVELATION 19:11

+

War and Military Intervention

The trinity of Richard Dawkins, Christopher Hitchens and
A. C. Grayling have come to a consensus – religion causes war.
Those who believe in God are too zealous and too quick to
fight others in order to enforce and impress their beliefs, or to
destroy those who don't agree with their religious way of life.

Unfortunately, such criticisms aren't without a certain element of truth. It would be a blinkered view of history that
didn't recognise the violence and bloodshed that has been
committed in the name of God, or that the borders of Christendom were both defended and expanded by the sword. Indeed,
'Christian nations' have even warred among themselves to try
to enforce doctrinal positions.

Today, of course, it is increasingly difficult to find Christians who would go to war to defend their religious beliefs or
to protect what they saw as the borders of a Christian nation.
But Christians are divided on the moral question as to whether
we should be involved in wars and the use of violence to defend
freedoms, ensure justice is maintained, protect the weak and
vulnerable, and to take a stand against our enemies.

It's a big question – with many shades, or nuances, of opinion. Some of the central issues involved from a Christian perspective are introduced and highlighted in the two contrasting letters below.

Dear Reader,

Military intervention is always the wrong option because God himself has refused it. Despite the appalling human evil in the world, the way in which God has intervened is through a Jewish Messiah who rejected violence (Luke 22:48-51; John 18:36). Despite human resistance to God's will, God sent his Son, not to enforce his rule, but to embody an alternative approach; a good life that challenged evil without replicating it. Despite our being enemies of God, we have been reconciled to God through the death of his Son, and we shall be saved by his life (Romans 5:8).

There is a powerful cultural myth that violence can be redemptive, that some evils can only be eradicated by force of arms. However, we have seen in Iraq and Afghanistan that military intervention creates at least as many problems as it appears to solve.

There will always be debate about whether military intervention 'works', but what should clinch the argument for Christians is the consistent New Testament teaching that God's character is fully revealed in Jesus of Nazareth, whose reconciling death has made peace (Colossians. 1:15–20), a peace that reaches across the most fundamental human divisions (Ephesians 2:14–17).

But is the Bible consistent? What can be said about the tension between the character of God as revealed by Jesus in the New Testament and some militaristic things said about God in the Old Testament?

When people first encounter God they may have distorted assumptions about this supernatural being. Thankfully God does not require someone to have a perfect theology before introducing himself. But neither is God content to allow those distorted assumptions about his character to remain; he wants us to get to know him better so that we can represent him faithfully.

Here is one example of God's gradual self-disclosure over time in the Old Testament; Abraham grew up in a culture that regarded child sacrifice as an appalling, though sometimes necessary, way to appeal for divine favour. The story of his near-offering of Isaac (Genesis 22:1–19) not only demonstrated his faith, it began a process of education marked by laws against child sacrifice (Deuteronomy 12:31; 18:10), and prophetic protestations against the very idea entering God's mind (Jeremiah 7:31; 19:5).

Although there are accounts of God commanding brutal conquest in the Old Testament, these cannot be maintained as revealing the final truth about God's character, even within the Old Testament, given its ultimate vision of peace (e.g., Isaiah 11:1–9). Indeed, the dominant Jewish tradition since A.D. 70 has been to reject violence since the rabbis taught that "the LORD is Peace" (Judges 6:24).

Jesus is God's final word about God's own character. He taught his disciples that peacemakers are called God's children (Matthew 5:9) and linked love of enemies directly to the character of our heavenly Father (Matthew 5:44-48). Followers of Jesus believe that the peace promised by the prophets has broken definitively into the middle of history, and thus refuse to perpetuate the cycle of violence through military intervention.

J.T. August 2009

Dear Reader,

A good friend was horrified when I announced God was calling me to become an Army chaplain. He was an intelligent, successful, Christian businessman. To him, the Armed Forces were the cause of violence not part of the solution. He felt the way of Christ was to abolish the military system. I believe that view is wrong and unbiblical.

When we think of military intervention, our minds often jump straight to full-scale war or armed conflict. The truth is, military intervention spans a whole spectrum between war, insurgency, post-conflict resolution, unrest, natural disasters and peace. Governments wield many 'levers' of power including diplomatic, economic and military measures. Military intervention is only one of those and is usually a last resort. However, many crises call for an international response where it is either too dangerous for civilian involvement or so chaotic that a disciplined military organisation delivers the best short-term solution till other agencies can follow.

What does the Bible say about military intervention, and particularly the use of military force? Biblical ethics are rooted not just in a few favourite verses but in the Bible's whole revelation of God's character and his plans for restoring the world in Christ. Is it ever right to go to war? Some people quote 'Thou shalt not kill' (Exodus 20:13) as if that said it all, forgetting that the very same writer sent an army to fight the Amalekites (chapter 17) and later gave instructions for the wholesale invasion of Canaan. The context is key. Exodus 20:13 deals with personal and social behaviour (specifically murder): it is not dealing with governments and war, other than to say that God bans the wrong use of force in taking life. Is there ever a right use?

We live in a sinful world. Jesus tells us there will always be 'wars and rumours of wars' while this world lasts (Matthew 24:4–8). The model God has put in place for leadership in both society and the church is based on his own character of justice and mercy. To act justly and to show mercy require defending the defenceless and delivering justice (Proverbs 31:8–9). What about Jesus' call to 'turn the other cheek' (Matthew 5:39)? He is speaking about personal behaviour, about response to personal wrongs. He is not suggesting that crime should go unpunished, otherwise law and order would break down. The civil authorities must at times use force, even lethal force, as God's representatives, for the preservation or restoration of peace (Romans 13:1–5; 1 Peter 2:13–14).

War is cruel and horrific; however, sometimes it is an unavoidable last resort. The principles that have been developed over the centuries (the Just War theory and the Law of Armed Conflict) are based on sound biblical principles of the minimal appropriate use of force, recognising that God created mankind in his own image. Military intervention spans a wide spectrum. Often, if we engage early enough at the appropriate lower level, we stand a chance of defusing what might otherwise degenerate into full-blown conflict. Finding the balance calls for the greatest of wisdom!

P.S. August 2009

+

Some Questions You Might Want to Think about and Discuss with Others

1. Should Christians ever be involved in acts of violence? How do you draw your conclusions?

2. 'Yahweh's association with the vengeance and violence of the Old Testament era wasn't an expression of who he was, so much as the result of his determination to be involved with his world. This unwillingness to distance himself

from the people of Israel and their actions meant that at times he became implicated in their excessive acts of violence.' What do you think of this assertion? Why? If true, what implications does this have for the way we view Christian involvement in violent conflict today?

3. How does the cross of Christ relate to this issue?

4. If Jesus had been employed as an advisor before the war in Iraq was declared, what advice do you think he would have given to Prime Minister Blair and President Bush?

5. What genuine alternatives are there to violence?

6. Would God rather see us use force or violence than see evil and injustice flourish?

part two

picture perfect

revolutionary

The writers of the New Testament are clear. God's character is fully, accurately and completely revealed by Jesus, who came, self-sacrificially served, died on the cross, rose again and sent the Holy Spirit to illumine, empower, guard and guide us. If you are looking for a master class in ethics, an advanced course in moral formation, the key to living beautifully – sign up here! Jesus is the picture of the way God is.

Judaism, into which Jesus was born, was seen as a 'way of life' in which one chose to walk, rather than a religion.[33] This is why the prophet Isaiah claimed of Yahweh's revelation to his people: 'This is the way; walk in it' (Isaiah 30:21).

But despite God's patience and the call of the prophets to stay faithful to Yahweh's character, Israel found herself, time and time again, all too easily drawn into the worship of other gods and the pursuit of other values. She constantly fell into the trap of acting in ways that distorted and polluted the transforming vision she was called to.

In this context, Jesus' words, 'I am the way and the truth and the life' (John 14:6) take on an extraordinarily dynamic and subversive edge. And of course, in exactly the same way, when the early Church designated their faith as 'The Way' it was just as revolutionary a statement.[34] 'Jesus Christ is the supreme act of divine intrusion into the world's settled arrangements. In ... Christ, God refuses to "stay in his place",' claim Stanley Hauerwas and William Willimon.[35]

It is not just that Jesus is the centre of our faith – but rather that his life, death, resurrection and ascension are the centre of history. Which, of course, is why we should be wary of any ethical schemes that do not need God to make themselves credible.

The Church is a community formed around the belief that Jesus Christ is the way, the truth and the life. We believe his story, which reveals to us who we are, what has happened in the world and where history is heading. Only on this basis can we answer the questions about how to behave. Our ethics are not just anyone's ethics with a little flavour of God thrown in. Our ethical positions and choices arise out of our commitment to Christ, and they are revolutionary. As Richard Lischer points out, 'Why should the Teacher be crucified for reinforcing what everyone already knows?'[36]

It is easy to assume that when we use words like *peace* and *justice* and *servanthood*, everyone knows what we are talking about and agrees with our definition, even if they don't know what it means that 'Jesus Christ is Lord'. All these big words, however, await definition and content. And for the Church they have little meaning apart from Christ's life, death and resurrection, which shape all our definitions. It is sobering to remember that Pilate permitted the killing of Jesus in order to secure peace and justice – Roman style – in Judea.

Beyond the Pale

The scribes and Pharisees didn't like the way that Jesus ignored their time-honoured interpretations of Scripture. As far as they were concerned, his views, indeed, his whole way of life, was blasphemous and heretical. And as a result, they wanted him silenced.

But as Seth Godin wittily remarks,

> We need heretics to keep faith alive.... Heretics are the people of faith who will risk everything to challenge the prevailing religion of the day.... By 'religion' I mean the rules and procedures that are in place. These rules were originally invented to amplify our faith, to make it easier to be passionate. But ... over time the rules get more solid and the faith begins to waver. That's why real change ... can only come from people with belief in the key mission and disrespect for the bureaucracy that has grown up over time.[37]

Perhaps that is why so many of the big human-rights advances we have witnessed over the years have been lead by those who, at the time, were widely written off as beyond the pale. It is only with hindsight that we recognise these were people who had the vision to see clearly, as well as the faith and courage to challenge the prevailing ethic – or orthodoxy – and bring about moral change. Take, for instance, William Wilberforce and the issue of slavery, Rev. Martin Luther King Jr and the long battle of the Civil Rights Movement, or Rev. Beyers Naude, the white South African Dutch Reformed Church leader who was expelled from his denomination for his early stance against Apartheid.

We do well if we also acknowledge and learn from the apathy and hostility these so-called heretics faced, not just from society in general, but to our shame, from large swathes of the Church. Indeed, history teaches us time and time again that even for the Church, one generation's heretic may turn out to be the next generation's prophet.

Being There

As the famous opening of John's gospel declares, 'The Word became a human being and lived here with us.... From him all the kindness and all the truth of God has come down to us' (John 1:14 CEV). Jesus is the Word (in Greek, *Logos)* of God – the ultimate revelator. Yahweh's full disclosure, or incarnation. And Jesus became the Logos in a specific time and place. That is what incarnation is. It is not a generalised concept – it is a specific, culturally bound action.

Through Jesus, God became a first-century, Aramaic speaking, olive-skinned, Palestinian carpenter. He grew up in an insubstantial town called Nazareth. He worked painstakingly to master a particular trade. His evenings were spent with a specific family and friends. He wept over the deaths of well-loved community members, hummed well-known tunes and laughed, over and over again, at his favourite jokes.

At about the age of thirty, he invested three years in teaching, healing, telling stories, asking questions, building relationships and mentoring a group of followers in and around the district of Galilee.

Finally, some three years later, he sacrificed his life through his death on a cross just outside the city of Jerusalem, on a Friday afternoon, and one and a half days later, early on Sunday morning, he rose from the dead in what was without doubt the most tumultuous weekend in history.

We believe in a God who was incarnated for thirty-three years, not just for three days! We believe in Jesus' life and teaching as well as his death and resurrection. The heart of the Bible's message about Jesus is built on a foundation of a life lived well, rather than simply the events of a long weekend.

To the extent that certain sections of the Church have – in their concern to make central what Jesus did for us through his death on the cross – downplayed this wider context, not only have we diminished him, but we have lost focus on so many of the questions that his life and teaching pose for the way we live day-to-day. And even more than that, we have been robbed of much of the depth of its impact in relation to culture and community, family and relationships, politics and economics, education and social justice, and even religion itself – not to mention the myriad other ethical and moral issues our culture faces.

So when Jesus said, if you're going to pray, pray this: 'Your will be done on earth as it is in heaven' (Matthew 6:10), the implication was this: Yahweh's holiness (his character) is made known in the world through the discipline of incarnation. But not just his – ours as well!

Holiness has to be embodied to be real or helpful. If we have seen Jesus, we know how God acts. We have had the chance to see, up close, his compassion and mercy and justice, his courage, patience, gentleness and love in action. We know what God looks like. As Jesus claimed: 'If you have seen me, you have seen the Father [God]' (John 14:9 CEV).

But the point is this: perhaps this is exactly what society should be able to say of those who follow him. As writer and theologian Gregory Boyd likes to say – and it's one of his favourite sayings – 'If it doesn't look like Jesus, it's not God!'

Story Time

Aristotle, the ancient philosopher, said that while history deals with facts, story deals with truth. And in ancient times, just like now, the primary teachers of morals were storytellers.

The stories they told encompassed everything: the origin of the world, how peoples and communities came into being, the rules and boundaries that determined society, the way to teach children ideas about love, life and death and how to become good members of that society.

Ancient storytellers, such as Aesop, famous for his fables, knew that a well-crafted story is a more powerful tool in terms of moral for- mation than any textbook on ethical theory. As the ethicist Alasdair MacIntyre wrote in his classic book *After Virtue*, 'Telling stories has a key part in educating us into the virtues.'[38]

In more recent times George Orwell, Aldous Huxley, J. R. R. Tolkien, C. S. Lewis and, today, the likes of J. K. Rowling have done much the same thing. Stories create whole worlds that we can enter through our imagination, learn from the virtues and vices of its characters and, therefore, understand, evaluate and redirect our own lives.

Unsurprisingly, much of Jesus' moral teaching came not in the form of command or succinct regulation, but in the form of stories. Jesus was a rabbi (a teacher). And rabbis were known for using the power of stories to engage their disciples in the learning process because 'it veiled the truth from frontal view,'[39] forcing them to think more deeply and use their imaginations to work out for themselves what an appropriate response would look like.

Imagination is far more central to developing the ability to live well than we have perhaps recognised. 'Forming the right kinds of instincts is really about developing the imagination.... Imagination ... is a key element in the moral life,' writes Samuel Wells.[40]

Imagination tends to be perceived as the opposite of morality. Morality is assumed to be about worthy but dull stuff, like fulfilling expectations, whereas imagination is associated with creativity, spontaneity and originality. For Jesus, however, the use of imagination was key to inspiring his hearers, as through his stories he invited them to imagine what a world, in which the rule of Yahweh is established, would look like and then commit to build it together.

Even when people asked Jesus direct questions about commands, he seldom opted for a straight yes or no because he knew that what really transforms the morality of individuals and, indeed, whole communities isn't a good grasp of the rules but the development of a good imagination.

There is no more obvious demonstration of Jesus' use of story to get people to see things differently than his encounter with an expert in the Law of Moses. The lawyer wants an answer to the question,

'Who are my neighbours?' (Luke 10:29 CEV). But there is more to all this than meets the eye. In truth, any Jewish expert in the Law would already have formed a very clear and set idea on the issue from their interpretation of the Scriptures.

Jesus was very aware of this. So, in response to the lawyer's question, he told one of his most well-known parables. The Good Samaritan, though brief, overflows with meaning, especially when understood within its original context.

As a man was going down from Jerusalem to Jericho, robbers attacked him and grabbed everything he had. They beat him up and ran off, leaving him half dead.

A priest happened to be going down the same road. But when he saw the man, he walked by on the other side. Later a temple helper came to the same place. But when he saw the man who had been beaten up, he also went by on the other side. A man from Samaria then came travelling along that road. When he saw the man, he felt sorry for him and went over to him. He treated his wounds with olive oil and wine and bandaged them. Then he put him on his own donkey and took him to an inn, where he took care of him. The next morning he gave the innkeeper two silver coins and said, 'Please take care of the man. If you spend more than this on him, I will pay you when I return.' (Luke 10:30–35 CEV)

Although there are three passers-by who see the victim of a robbery, Jesus' story boils down to two opposing types of response.

First, that of the priest and the Levite. Both see the man but choose to pass by and do nothing – why? Well, surprisingly the answer lies in an ethical dilemma he posed to them, brought about by their understanding of the Law, which they believed had been given to them by God. Kenneth Bailey, an expert in Middle Eastern culture, comments of the priest,

No doubt, [he] wanted to do his duty under the Law. But what was his duty?...

The wounded man could have been dead. If so the priest who approached him would become ceremonially defiled, and if defiled he would need to return to Jerusalem and undergo a week-long process of ceremonial purification.... What's more, the victim along the road might have been Egyptian, Greek, Syrian or Phoenician, in which case, the priest was not responsible under the law to do anything.... The poor priest did not have an easy time trying to determine his duty under the law. After deciding that his ceremonial purity was too important to risk, he continued on his way.[41]

Then, by contrast, a Samaritan (a despised and hated outsider in the eyes of the Jews, especially the experts in the Law) sees the victim lying in the road and is moved by compassion. This twist in the story would have not only shocked but thoroughly scandalised both the lawyer and Jesus' wider audience, who at the very least would have expected an ordinary Jew – like one of them – to come to the aid of the victim.

Unfortunately, due to ideas that the priest and Levite got from their misunderstanding of the moral law they were trying so earnestly to live by, 'the Samaritan', writes William Spohn, 'sees the man as a fellow human being in terrible trouble. [Their] perception was funded by categories of corpse, Gentile and defilement.'[42]

In the original Greek, the word that Jesus chooses to use explains that the Samaritan felt *esplanchnisthe* for the mugger's victim, which expresses a sense of deep compassion from the core of his being. Jesus was saying that the Samaritan's action was the result of being in touch with, and listening to, the soul-shaking emotion that was part of his moral fabric and which left him in no doubt as to how he should respond. 'Practices are manifestations of one's character,' observes New Testament scholar Joel Green.[43]

The Samaritan was moved by empathy and concern for the person in need rather than blinded by the baggage of his misinterpretation of religious moral laws. But what is more, his concern was no fleeting sentiment. As Jesus explained, it also looked beyond this victim's immediate need to the ongoing issues that he might face.

With the story told, Jesus circles round and returns to the lawyer's original question, Who is my neighbour? Yet, instead of simply repeating it, he seizes the initiative, flips it and asks the lawyer a similar but different question: 'Which one of these three people was a real neighbour to the man who was beaten up by robbers?' (Luke 10:36 CEV). To which the only answer – even from the legal expert – is 'The one who showed pity.'

Jesus tells this parable to illustrate to the expert in the Law that his moral categories are too rigid. The lawyer's original question had simply been an attempt to establish the boundaries of his legal responsibilities: 'Whom do I have to love?', 'Do I have to literally love everyone as I love myself?', 'Do I have to love all foreigners or just foreigners who have become part of our community?', 'What about our enemies, the Romans? Or people we despise, like Samaritans – do I seriously have to love them?'

Jesus' point is this. The expert's interpretation of the Law has boxed him in and, ironically, blinded him to its whole purpose. Not only has it shrunk his moral vision, but made it quite 'un-Yahweh-like'.

Jesus wants him to see things differently – which is why he turns the question on its head to illustrate the real intention of the Law and get right to the heart of who we are as human beings.

The real issue for Jesus isn't about legal categories to define the word *neighbour*, but about our character and response when faced with human need. It's the difference between looking for the limitations of duty as set out by a rulebook approach to faith and morality, and seeing things differently – with the eyes of Yahweh.

Through the telling of a well-chosen story, Jesus paints a picture of a moral vision about what life looks like when it is lived with Yahweh's compassion. A picture of what it is to be holy as God is holy. What he hasn't done, however, is give the lawyer a new rule that he can then abstract, systematise and police.

Dependent

One of the criticisms and concerns of those who fear emphasising character and instinct rather than rules in the pursuit of developing morality is the fear that we might easily fall into the trap of believing that we have the ability to be moral and make ethical decisions based on our own resources – *independently* of God.

In reality, the reverse is true. As Jesus' life and teaching highlight, our ability to make the right decisions is utterly dependant on the depth of our relationship with, and experience of, God, which, as he explains, must be more profound than a detached, textbook knowledge of Scripture, however comprehensive that might be. 'For I tell you that unless your righteousness surpasses that of the Pharisees and the teachers of the Law, you will certainly not enter the kingdom of heaven' (Matthew 5:20).[44]

The gospel writers reveal that Jesus was able to act in line with Yahweh's character – showing compassion and mercy, justice and forgiveness – because of his dependence on the Holy Spirit. More than that, they depict him as 'developing' and 'growing' in wisdom, as he was obedient to his Father and guided by the Holy Spirit.[45]

And what is true for Jesus, is also true for us. Our becoming moral persons – truly Christ-like human beings – is only made possible through a living relationship with his Spirit, who develops in us a moral character based on virtues that are at the heart of who God is, expressed in the life of Jesus.[46] As Paul writes to the church at Galatia, 'God's Spirit makes us loving, happy, peaceful, patient, kind, good, faithful, gentle, and self-controlled' (Galatians 5:22–23 CEV).

Despite the fact that humanity is clearly advancing scientifically, medically and technologically with great speed, we don't (and never will) have the power, skill or ability to create through our own resources a genuinely good way of being – or seeing differently – without demonstrating the same dependence on God.

As Jesus himself promised, 'I will ask the Father to send you the Holy Spirit who will help you and always be with you. The Spirit will show you what is true ... and will keep on living in you' (John 14:16–17 CEV). As the apostle Paul wrote in his letter to the Philippians, 'God is the one who began this good work in you, and ... he won't stop before it is complete' (Philippians 1:6 CEV).

Good Habits

Our developing character is a gift of God's Spirit – an act of his grace. But we are also asked to work to be part of this development.

Paul wrote, 'God is working in you to make you willing and able to obey him' (Philippians 2:13 CEV). But Peter added; 'Do your best to improve your faith ... by adding goodness, understanding, self-control, patience, devotion to God, concern for others, and love' (2 Peter 1:5–7 CEV).

Hard ethical judgements and choices face our society in the years ahead as we attempt to make big decisions. Who will have medical treatment and who will not? What rights does a person have to restrict access to their genetic information? Are genetically engineered crops ethically justifiable? Can living wills by patients who are terminally ill and in great pain justify bringing their lives to an end? How and for what reasons should criminals be punished? Should the powers of the media be curbed? Not only is the list of questions lengthy but, of course, at this point in time, many of the answers are unwritten.

Equally, from time to time, each one of us finds ourselves faced with some kind of big and difficult decision.

If we only think of ethics as debating the big issues, however, such as those to do with medicine, international justice, the environment, the economy, business, education and poverty, and dealing with moments of personal crisis, we make a huge mistake.

It seems strange to say it, but ethics is about much more than all that. For all those who follow Christ, ethics is not about isolated actions or big decisions, but about the whole process of becoming the sort of person God wills us to be and commits himself to making us.

Ethics are essentially about everyday life – our passions and perceptions – and the slow cultivation of good habits and moral skills. All of which means that, in short, every moment, even the most mundane, is an opportunity for moral formation and development.

On Thursday, 15 January 2009, Flight 1549 took off from LaGuardia, New York, heading for North Carolina with 155 passengers and crew on board. Just one minute into the flight, the plane experienced a massive bird strike and all power was lost in both engines.

Faced with a pilot's worst nightmare, Captain Chesley Sullenberger contacted the ground and weighed up his options. Almost immediately it was obvious that a return to LaGuardia wasn't on the cards. With further assessment, neither was the short flight to Teteboro, New Jersey. So, with time running out and a calmness that revealed nothing of his inner turmoil, Captain Sullenberger spoke what most assumed would be his last words: 'We'll be in the Hudson.'

The fact that Flight 1549 landed on the Hudson River in one piece, without loss of life or serious injury, was deemed nothing short of a miracle – and in some ways it was. But as Sullenberger revealed in an interview a few weeks later, he wasn't praying during those five short minutes – 'I assumed others were taking care of that.' What he was doing was responding to a unique situation as if it happened all the time.

After forty years as a pilot, Sullenberger reacted to the dilemma facing him as if it was second nature. His decision to ditch in the Hudson River wasn't made because the rules told him that was the right thing to do. Neither was he making the decision based on the possible consequences of doing so – after all, planes are not designed to land on water, and most attempts have ended in complete catastrophe.

What allowed Captain Sullenberger to make the decision that turned out to be the 'miracle on the Hudson', was forty years of experience, training and discipline. Through hundreds and hundreds of flying hours, he had developed a set of habits and skills that, though now second nature to him, allowed him to make decisions that were not the obvious choices to make nor the ones that his pilot's manual would have told him to choose.

Moral success is every bit as much about the formation of good habits over time and through disciplined effort, as any other skill. And the point of all this training and discipline is that on the day – at the moment of decision – you do the right things naturally.

We have reduced ethics to the moment of decision – the attempt to negotiate hopelessly difficult moral dilemmas – and that is our biggest problem! As Samuel Wells says, 'The moral life should not be experienced as an agony of impossible choices. It should be a matter of habit and instinct. Learning to live well is about developing the right instincts and habits.'[47]

Some years ago I saw the following anonymous quotation written on a wall in a school:

Watch your thoughts, they become words.
Watch your words, they become actions.
Watch your actions, they become habits.
Watch your habits, they become your character.
Watch your character, it becomes your destiny.

Every athlete knows that the race is won or lost at the training ground before it is ever won or lost in the stadium. A world-class 100-meter sprinter will train for years for a race that will last under ten seconds. Success is the result of skill gained through disciplined training and sacrifice. And no amount of enthusiasm on the 'big day' will ever make up for the deficiencies in that training and preparation. As Wells says,

> Training requires commitment, discipline, faithfulness, study, apprenticeship, practice, cooperation, observation, reflection – in short, moral effort. The point of this effort is to form skills and habits – habits that mean people take the right things for granted and skills that give them ability to do the things they take for granted.[48]

The problem is that the way most people think about ethics neglects the only time we can use to make a real difference – in the crisis, only the habits we have already formed can help us. In fact, many of the impossibly big decisions we face wouldn't arise at all if we had a different ethical foundation in the first place.

The great majority of life is spent in preparation – so that is where the emphasis needs to be. Just as the athlete, through disciplined training, develops physical reflexes, our ethical task is to develop the equivalent moral reflexes. As the saying goes, success is 10 percent inspiration and 90 percent perspiration.

In the film *Evan Almighty*, God (played by Morgan Freeman) decides to give Congressman Evan Baxter a real chance to live up to his campaign slogan, 'Change the World', by telling Evan that he has to build an ark, just like the one Noah built, as there is going to be a huge flood coming. Evan builds the ark, but the pressures of the task take their toll on his family life. In one scene from the film, Evan's wife is sitting in a restaurant and calls over the waiter – who just happens to be 'God', though of course she isn't aware of this. She and God get into a conversation about the 'ridiculous' boat-building scheme that

Evan is convinced God has asked him to do. His wife doesn't get it, but 'God' has a different take on the situation:

> If someone prays for patience, do you think God gives them patience? Or does he give them the opportunity to be patient? If they pray for courage, does God give them courage or does he give them the opportunity to be courageous? If someone prayed for their family to be closer, do you think God zaps them with warm fuzzy feelings? Or does he give them opportunities to love each other?[49]

Living beautifully turns out to be about the discipline of slowly developing the right kinds of habits and instincts. For those who fail to cultivate such ethical reflexes, all too often the tough decisions that arise are insoluble, whereas, for those who through discipline have acquired the necessary skills, many of the situations others experience as crises of choice pass by unnoticed.

Or to put it another way – holiness is a habit, not a performance.

chosen

It's a dilemma – a mystery that so many find impossible to solve.

On one hand, as Jesus himself explained it, 'Don't suppose that I came to do away with the Law and the Prophets. I did not come to do away with them, but to give them their full meaning' (Matthew 5:17 CEV).

But on the other hand, he announces ...

> You have been taught that a man who divorces his wife must write out divorce papers for her. But I tell you not to divorce your wife unless she has committed some terrible sexual sin. . . .
>
> You know that our ancestors were told, 'Don't use the Lord's name to make a promise unless you are going to keep it.' But I tell you not to swear by anything when you make a promise! . . .
>
> You know that you have been taught, 'An eye for an eye and a tooth for a tooth.' But I tell you not to try to get even with a person who has done something to you. . . .
>
> You have heard people say, 'Love your neighbours and hate your enemies.' But I tell you to love your enemies and pray for anyone who mistreats you. (Matthew 5:31–32, 33–34, 38–39, 43–44 CEV)

And then there is Jesus' deliberately renegade attitude to the Sabbath, to eating with 'sinners', to the Temple laws, to non-Jews, to the Roman occupation and countless other issues which increasingly got under the skin of Israel's teachers.

Fulfilment

Jesus' Sermon on the Mount (Matthew 5–7), one of the most famous passages in the New Testament, is filled with what we would call moral, or ethical, teaching. Though put more straightforwardly, it is a vision for what it means to be human and live beautifully. 'People often say what wonderful teaching the Sermon on the Mount is,' observes N. T. Wright, 'and that if only people would obey it the world would be a better place. But if we think of Jesus simply sitting there, telling people how to behave properly, we will miss what was really going on.'[50]

The last thing that the ordinary people of Jesus' time needed was a new set of rules and tougher standards to try to live up to. They were already staggering under the burden of trying to cope with the exacting interpretation of the Law of Moses, which the Pharisees and other religious leaders presented to them as nonnegotiable.

Jesus' contention wasn't that there was a problem with the Law as such. The problem was that the religion of the scribes and Pharisees – whose whole approach was based on endless rules and regulations – had twisted, warped and hidden God's real character (the essence of the Law and Prophets) from the ordinary people, rather than revealing him to them. Instead of providing the basis for liberation, the religious leaders' whole method of interpreting the Torah[51] had become a tool of condemnation, oppression, rejection and exclusion.

As we've already seen, once you get wrapped up in a pedantic and time-bound rulebook approach to life, insisting that obedience to every detail is the only legitimate means of moral formation, the bigger vision of life lived God's way is inevitably lost – or as Jesus puts it in his sermon, 'You end up building on sand – the kind of stuff that people sink in – rather than rock' (see Matthew 7:24–27), concluding that, 'Anyone who hears and obeys these teachings of mine is like a wise person who built his house on solid rock' (Matthew 7:24 CEV).

As Jesus was quick to explain to his audience, rather than planning to do away with or replace the Law, his goal was simple: to give it its full meaning – and this he would do, not just by unpacking and explaining it, but by reframing it.

The development of a healthy spirituality, one that reflects rather than distorts God, is not primarily about rules, but about vision. Only this provides a strong enough motive for the formation of the habits and practices that give rise to the ability to be the kind of person who echoes God's character. Religion, on the other hand, under the 'yoke' of the leaders of Jesus' day, had become nothing more than a set of regulations. The Torah had been reduced to a book of limitations. They had turned God's Law into an elaborate list of dos and don'ts – inflexible and narrow-minded regulations – that governed their responses to any and every situation, blinkered their thinking and created an impossible but worthless burden for the ordinary people.

How often has the Church been trapped into promoting exactly this same understanding?

I recall a friend of mine telling me about the approach to life within his denomination: 'It seems as though we have a position on everything,' he observed. 'And by becoming a leader within it you are forced to comply.... There is no discussion. You tow the line or you become *persona non grata.*'

Of course, it's not just the Church that acts this way. Consider the office handbook. How many of us work in situations filled with rules that are just plain stupid, yet they remain in place. They frustrate people, cause tension, cost time, cost money and squander goodwill. So, why do they exist? Because once, maybe a long time ago, in a specific situation or set of circumstances, each one of them made sense. They were put in place to protect an ethos, a vision; but now, not only do they dominate, frustrate and crush people instead of serving them, they rob them of the very passion that once motivated them.

Did you know that in the UK today, unrepealed ancient laws mean that:

- It is still an act of treason to place a postage stamp bearing the British monarch upside down – a law passed in 1840 to stop people 'insulting the monarchy' when the first Penny Black stamp was issued.
- That all Englishmen over the age of fourteen are still required to spend two hours a week practising the longbow, supervised by local clergy.

Whereas, in North America:

- Anyone who detonates a nuclear device in the city limits in Chico, California, can be fined $500.
- The entire *Encyclopaedia Britannica* is banned in Texas because it contains a formula for making beer at home.[52]

What these and many other laws have in common is that they made real sense to someone when they were passed, but now, in the context of a changed world, they have become irrelevant – or even worse. The law, as they say, has become an ass.

Inside Out

Jesus' point, however, is deeper still. It's not just that the scribes and Pharisees have the wrong rules, and that if they could be persuaded to adopt some better ones, all would be well. It's that a rulebook approach – *any* rulebook approach – to trying to represent God just does not work.

Jesus' sermon is not designed to provide a better set of rules, but instead to articulate core principles that comprise God's character and demonstrate his nature. The intention of the Sermon on the Mount is not to set out a list of immoveable one-size-fits-all regulations, but rather to establish a framework for the development of moral skills and habits based on the character of God. As William Spohn puts it: '[Jesus] commends specific dispositions of the heart that produce a more profound obedience: mercy, gratitude, radical trust in God, and non-discriminatory love. Behavioural commands cannot get to heart of the matter.'[53]

That's just it! You can keep all your rules, all of the time, yet still be of morally dubious character. You may not actually ever be violent – but your soul may be full of hatred, rage and violence. You may never commit a physical act of adultery, but that doesn't mean that within your heart you haven't grown unfaithful. You can give money to charity, but lack any kind of generosity of spirit. You can do the chores, without the heart of a servant. You can fulfil the technical requirements of the letter of the law, but never even come close to beginning to tackle the real issues at the heart of bringing God's kingship to earth. As Jesus put it elsewhere:

> You give God a tenth of the spices from your garden, such as mint, dill, and cumin. Yet you neglect the more important matters of the Law, such as justice, mercy, and faithfulness.... You wash the outside of your cups and dishes, while inside there is nothing but greed and selfishness.... First clean the inside of a cup, and then the outside will also be clean.... You're like tombs that have been whitewashed. On the outside they are beautiful, but inside they are full of bones and filth. That's what you are like. Outside you look good, but inside you are evil and only pretend to be good. (Matthew 23:23–28 CEV)

Unlike some members of modern-day church congregations, no one on that mountain, that day, had to be there. Not one person in Jesus' hillside audience turned up out of a sense of obligation, duty or habit. Nobody was forcing them to attend – it wasn't *expected* of them. 'I've spent my life trying to get people to come and hear me,' observed Dallas Willard in his book *The Divine Conspiracy*, 'but when I look at Jesus, his problem was getting away from people!'[54]

So, what was it that was so compelling about Jesus' teaching? Why were the disenfranchised and the 'sermoned-out' so keen to crowd around him? What was it about his words that stood in such stark contrast to those of all the other rabbis and religious teachers of his day?

These people came to listen to Jesus because they wanted to. His message was, quite simply, the best thing they had ever heard – it was 'good news', rather than another dose of the bad news and condemnation that they were so used to having hurled at them from their religious leaders, or, even worse, a set of new and *even more* rigorous laws.

Jesus' sermon is really the public announcement of how things are now that the Kingdom of God is breaking into the world, and God is taking control. 'The Kingdom is here,' was Jesus' constant refrain.[55] And through it, he unpacks his compelling vision for life – a vision, which over the next three years, he would systematically live out. But more than that, he issues an open invitation to all people to choose to join in and become citizens of this new Kingdom, where God's will is being done on earth as it is in heaven.

Developing a healthy ethic is, first, about understanding 'who you are'. Only this approach can create an adequate base for the subsequent discussions of 'how to behave' or 'what you do (or don't do) in any given situation'. And this explains why Jesus begins his sermon not by telling his audience what to do, but with the Beatitudes – helping them to see who they really are.

God blesses you who are spiritually poor.... God blesses the hungry.... God blesses those of you who are crying.... (Matthew 5:3–12).

And as Jesus made these extraordinary statements and looked out on the crowd of ordinary people that surrounded him, many of whom he would have recognised,[56] he announced, 'God's Kingdom belongs to you!'

Jesus was not saying, as so often suggested, that if you work yourself into one of these conditions you are somehow better in the eyes of God. He wasn't saying, 'Get poor! Start mourning now! Get yourself persecuted if you want to know God's blessing!' To think of Jesus' teaching in this way would reduce it to nothing more than another dose of salvation by works. And this wouldn't have been good news; but rather more backbreaking, soul-destroying, bad news.

So, why were the people in these categories Jesus named blessed? They were blessed not because of their attainment but simply because of God's generosity. 'The Beatitudes are not a strategy for achieving a better society, they are an indication, a picture, a vision of the in-breaking of a new society,' claim Stanley Hauerwas and William Willimon.[57]

Jesus never suggests his Beatitudes are an exhaustive list, however; rather they are merely examples of the oppressed, excluded and misunderstood of his day. His message was simply, 'Blessed are you, because God is on your side – his Kingdom belongs to you!'

This same message runs consistently through the Gospels. Cut into the accounts of Jesus' life at any point and you will see the same thing writ large and bold. Those who had previously been excluded have now become the unexpected recipients of the good news. As Jesus himself explains to the followers of John the Baptist, 'The poor are hearing the good news' (Matthew 11:5 CEV).

In Jesus, the Kingdom of God has arrived, and the previous measuring rod that the religious authorities have used, based on their legalistic, negative and misguided reading of the Law of Moses, is being replaced.

Does God Believe in Me?

If Jesus' Sermon on the Mount had ended with his list of revolutionary Beatitudes, that would have been radical enough, challenging as it did the current social and religious systems, and offering hope to countless numbers of disenfranchised Jews. But he hadn't finished yet.

Before his audience could catch their breath, Jesus had launched straight into yet another groundbreaking set of statements. Rather than attempting to tell them off or frighten them into following him, he astonishes them by declaring, 'You are the salt of the earth.' And then, 'You are the light of the world' (Matthew 5:13, 14).

It's hard to imagine how that would have made them feel. 'Us? Salt? We've always been told we were scum!' There must have been large numbers of people who sat on that hillside with huge smiles, chuckling to themselves that day – as their emotions oscillated between a sense of sheer relief and lingering disbelief.

Jesus came to help people to see the world with different eyes; to understand that they were blessed by God – and as a result, to empower them to live that way. And in this task he consistently refused to employ the sin-management technique of nagging and yelling at people. He believed in the carrot, not the stick. He knew how to draw people to him rather than drive them away.

Jesus refused to push, force, bludgeon, beat, coerce, cajole, manhandle or bully his audience into following him. Condemnation and judgement were the wrong tools for his task.

The question the crowd brought to Jesus was not 'Do I believe in God?' Beaten down, as the people were, by the demands of the religious leaders, the deepest question of their hearts had become, 'Does God believe in me?' Jesus' answer to their question is an emphatic and affirming 'Yes!' In the words of Psalm 34:18 (NIrV): 'The Lord is close to those whose hearts have been broken. He saves those whose spirits have been crushed.'

Jesus' sermon is, first and foremost, a description of the way God is. And his challenge is this: 'If you believe that this is the way that Yahweh is and, therefore, that this is the way that the world is, then the way that you choose to live should reflect that.'

'You are the salt of the earth,' he taught them but added, 'if that salt loses its saltiness what is it good for?'

The Way Things Are

If Jesus' sermon is not a new set of more stringent rules for us to observe, but rather a picture of the way God is, it changes everything.

If we live in a world where only the strong, the powerful, the rich, the independent and the successful are blessed by God, then, like it or not, we have to at least accept it and, perhaps, even learn to swim with the tide. But if it is true that the world is actually a place where God is on the side of – and blesses – the poor and the hungry, that means that we should get in step or else live our whole lives at odds with the way things actually are.

We seek reconciliation with our neighbour not primarily because it will make us feel so much better afterwards (it may or it may not!). We seek reconciliation with our neighbour because that reflects who God is – the great reconciler. Therefore, instead of responding to Jesus' teaching by asking 'Is this a practical way to live?' the question becomes, 'Is this really the way the world is?'

So it is that Jesus inspires us to 'be perfect, therefore, as your heavenly Father is perfect' (Matthew 5:48) – to be different the way that God is different. We aim to live generously because God is generous; to live faithfully because God is faithful; to live as peacemakers because God is the peacemaker.

But Jesus does not claim that his teaching is common sense or that it will make sense to everybody. Nothing in his sermon suggests that his way of discipleship is 'rational', as seen through the eyes of others. In fact, he openly admits that his teaching goes against everything his audience had ever heard. 'You have heard it said ...' is, of course, a reference to the Law of Moses – the Torah. As Hauerwas and Willimon remind us:

> It might be possible for Christians to argue that our ethics are universally applicable, that the way of Jesus makes sense even to those who do not believe that the claim 'Jesus Christ is Lord' makes sense. Christians could then join hands with all people of goodwill who want peace, who work for justice, who affirm life, and who strive for the good ... [that is] until we collide with a text like Jesus' Sermon on the Mount. There, even the most casual observer realises that he or she has been confronted by a way that does not make sense. In the Sermon on the Mount, the boundaries between church and world are brought into clear relief.[58]

Those who choose this narrow way – who are determined to walk the way of the Kingdom rather than the wide road that leads to destruction – may well be laughed at by others for 'taking it all too far', for getting things out of proportion, for being fanatical, idealistic or naïve. Indeed, as Jesus indicated, they may even face persecution and rejection.

It is just that if Jesus' way is the way that God is, it is not only shortsighted but stupid to live any other way, because it is to live out of step with the way that the world actually is.

Learning Jazz

The Pharisees were worried that if you give up on the rules – on the positions you held – you would be giving up on discipleship. But discipleship is not primarily about rules; it's about the development of habits and practices. You learn a skill when you are inspired by a vision. Kids become great footballers because they dream of being like their heroes. It is this vision that drives them to spend hour after hour kicking a ball up against a wall or learning to juggle the ball.

Oasis, the organisation I work for, runs schools in various countries around the world. One of the big questions we constantly wrestle with is how to teach spirituality without it descending into religion. How many people do you know that went to a religious school and, as a result, have never set a foot in a church building since?

The problem is that it is so easy to set out to teach spirituality and to end up teaching religion by mistake. Religion – in terms of the popular understanding of the term, rather than its true meaning[59] – is what you end up with when you try to encode spirituality.

So, while Jesus honours the Torah, he wants to dig deeper. Through a series of well-chosen illustrations, he pushes his audience to think about what they have been taught about the Law in the light of the vision he is presenting to them of who Yahweh actually is.

He provocatively pushes his audience beyond their rules to the underlying principles behind them; he is asking that they let go of their legalism and live radically.

In order to do this, Jesus cites a series of older commands – from the Torah – about murder, adultery, divorce, oaths, revenge and attitudes to enemies, and then sets about radically deepening their significance (see Matthew 5:21–48). None of this is to lay some gigantic ethical burden on the backs of his hearers – and they didn't understand it that way. Rather, Jesus is creating a series of imaginative metaphors, with which he hopes to prod their imaginations – a series of examples of life lived God's way, which are designed to inspire further thought about their lives and responses.

Rather than living by the rules – that is, taking them at face value and mindlessly applying them without thought of their original context or purpose – Jesus was demonstrating that what God really wants is for people to live within the spirit of the rules.

It's rather like the difference between someone who can read music and so is able to play the tune they see written down in front of them, and a jazz musician who understands the structures and principles and roots behind the tune and so develops the ability to improvise with great skill in harmony with it.

One person is restricted by the rules. The other is set free by them. One person has to do exactly the same thing in exactly the same way every time because they have no choice. While the other person has the skill, the confidence and the framework to improvise; to be set free by the music rather than imprisoned within it.

In other words, Jesus is trying to get people to recognise that the rules themselves may not always be relevant in every time and place or, indeed, that there may not be an actual rule we can point to for the situation we are facing. However, the principles behind the rules – such as mercy, justice, faithfulness, generosity, compassion, fortitude, patience, integrity and wisdom – are constantly applicable to life because they flow from the story of the giver of life: God himself.

It's about depth of character rather than breadth of knowledge – as Jesus so often tries to get the scribes and Pharisees to see.

Written in Sand

A fascinating and important encounter that clearly demonstrates Jesus' radically different understanding of the Law of Moses (the Torah) and the moral vision behind it, takes place between Jesus and a Jewish mob who had brought a woman to him who they claimed had been caught in the act of adultery (John 8:1–11): 'The Law of Moses teaches that a woman like this should be stoned to death! What do you say?' (John 8:5 CEV).

The Pharisees were looking for Jesus to either agree with them and the Law of Moses or to try to wriggle out and compromise it. The backdrop to the story, however, is that in the current political climate the Jews weren't actually allowed to put anyone to death, whatever the Law of Moses said.[60]

So what does Jesus do?

He bends down and starts to write in the dust – which seems like a strange and pointless action. Was he playing for time? Was he doodling so as to gather his thoughts?

From the surrounding narrative, we know this was the first day after the Festival of Shelters, which meant it was governed by Sabbath law, and, therefore, strictly speaking, you had to refrain from all work. And for the Pharisees watching on, that includes writing.

As Kenneth Bailey points out, however, the Pharisees had definitions for everything, and in their hair-splitting world, writing was defined as 'making some kind of permanent mark'; therefore, 'writing with one's finger in the dust was permissible because [according to the Mishnah] it "leaves no lasting mark".'[61]

Jesus was not playing for time. Rather, he was making it clear to the Pharisees that he not only knew the written law, but that he was as fully aware of the convoluted nuances of the oral tradition and the current interpretations of it, as they were. If they want to play games of textual interpretation he is their match.

John does not record what Jesus actually wrote in the sand – it is only open to speculation. (Though, the fact that it is not recorded should perhaps convince us that it is unimportant to the story.) What Jesus says in response to his questioners, however, is masterful: 'If any of you have never sinned, then go ahead and throw the first stone at her!' (John 8:7 CEV).

Rather than answer their question on their terms, Jesus changes the emphasis and direction of the conversation. In doing so, he refuses to let the Pharisees hide behind the rules. Instead of responding to the question of whether stoning the woman is against the Law, he holds up a mirror to them and confronts them with their own moral character. In this way, Jesus raises the question as to whether any of them are morally superior to this adulteress; and whether any of them have actually got the courage to follow through on the religious convictions they spend their whole lives flaunting by implementing the full penalty of the law – as they see it – against the will of the Romans. Which of course, they haven't!

As Kenneth Bailey suggests, all through this encounter 'Jesus is subtly debating the nature of justice. Is justice primarily a strict application of law, important though that may be? Or must the prophetic definition of justice found in the Servant Songs of Isaiah be considered?'[62] As Isaiah defines it, 'He won't break off a bent reed or put out a dying flame, but he will make sure that justice is done' (Isaiah 42:3 CEV).

The Pharisees 'see' the letter of the Law and want it to be fulfilled. Jesus sees the woman, the broken reed, and wants the deeper principle of justice, articulated by Isaiah, to be worked out in her situation.

The Pharisees have learnt the tune, but Jesus plays jazz.

But having demonstrated how morally wrong the crowd was to look for justice according to the rules, at no point does Jesus condone or defend the actions of the woman, even though he clearly finds no purpose in condemning her.

Instead, what he is doing, both to the crowd and to the woman, is to raise the fundamentally more vital question about their moral character. So, he turns and addresses the woman. 'Go now and leave your life of sin.' Why? Because her actions, just as those of her accusers, break with the character of God.

Jesus is teaching everyone to play jazz.

thinking christianly

You may say to yourself, 'My power and the strength of my hands have produced this wealth for me.' But remember the LORD your God, for it is he who gives you the ability to produce wealth.

DEUTERONOMY 8:17–18

+

The Use of Wealth

In the Bible, wealth, poverty and justice are inextricably linked. Page after page of the Old Testament Law and much of the prophetic tradition are given over to such issues. In the teachings of Jesus, there is far more about money and how we use it than almost any subject – including sexuality. And yet, our fixation with the latter often distracts us from seriously engaging with the former with the same rigour that Jesus and the moral vision of the Old Testament suggest we should.

With the almost total collapse of Communism in the late eighties and early nineties, our world is now dominated by market economies. For some, though imperfect, this is the best system we have for controlling and sharing wealth nationally and globally. For others, such a system favours a few at the expense of the majority and is the cause of much injustice.

So, how should Christians respond to and live within a market economy, and can such a system be in line with the moral vision of God?

The following letters are written by Christians who work in the political/public sphere and have commitments to seeing a

Christian moral vision lived out in those areas. As you will see, however, they represent two very different points of view – and, of course, are just two opinions in a much larger debate.

Dear Reader,

It's always tempting to try to legitimate one's prejudices or political philosophy with a bit of theology, whether it be the Socialism of the 1960s or the ideology of the American Religious Right. The opposite temptation, of course, is to accept the enlightenment heresy of a split-level universe where God belongs 'upstairs' and society, politics and everything else that really matters is kept downstairs. Like the scrapbooks in the attic, it's reassuring to know that God is 'up there', but we don't let him impact our public lives and certainly not our politics. Christianity rejects both approaches. Certainly, faith is personal, but it can never be private. The challenge is to ensure that good theology and an understanding of God's character shape our perspectives on everything.

A free economy is one where individuals and families are free, under the rule of law, to act to use their economic resources as they wish to achieve their own objectives (which may not be material objectives: I may use my time to do some voluntary work, for example, which is an economic resource being used for purely charitable objectives). The market part of the free economy (and, therefore, a market economy) is one where individuals and families, under the rule of law, are free to participate in a process of economic exchange, using their economic resources to achieve their own defined objectives. This is often contrasted with a planned economy, in which a central government determines the price of goods and services using a fixed price system. It's important not to idolise the free market, but there are some good theological arguments in support of it.

Freedom is a core theme – freedom from authoritarian con-
straints and the freedom to be human. The market economy
recognises the importance of human freedom and the dignity of
every human being. It's generally better at securing the necessary
conditions for the common good than the alternative economic
models available. It's not perfect because humans aren't. The market economy's a bit like democracy. Churchill once quipped that
'democracy is the worst form of government except for all the others that have been tried.'

God allows human beings significant freedom, based on their
innate dignity. In the beginning God created human beings in 'his
image' and commanded them to rule the earth accordingly on
his behalf. In the event, human beings defied their Creator and
rebelled against him. In his governance of the universe, therefore,
God acknowledges the importance of freedom. Similarly, the free
market allocates resources through voluntary contract whereas
government allocates resources through force of law.

The Role of the Governing Authorities

In the New Testament, the apostle Paul also recognises the importance of freedom. The role of the governing authorities, he argues, is
to restrain evil (and punish it) and to secure the conditions (infrastruc-
ture) for the possibility of the common good (Romans 13:1–7).

The Limits of Government

It's a heresy to believe that either the state or the market can
solve every problem or deliver the good of society directly. Critically,
there is also a third sector. The governing authorities should be
kept in their proper place. Government shouldn't usurp the role of
families, congregations, faith communities, fellowships, neighbour-
hoods and voluntary organisations.

The Common Good

The market economy is better at enabling the common good to be secured. For example, less-efficient economic systems produce less while using more resources; people are poorer as a result. The poor tend to be much poorer in socialist economic systems than in market oriented ones.

Freedom with a Moral and Legal Context

Of course, like all freedoms, the freedom of the market economy cannot be absolute. The market economy, like individuals, must operate within a moral framework and the rule of law.

The Difference between Self-Interest and Greed

One final point: the market economy assumes self-interest. However, self-interest is not the same as greed or selfishness. I choose to cycle or walk to work rather than take a car, bus or train. In doing so, I am acting according to self-interest, but it's got nothing to do with being greedy.

In summary, the market economy recognises the importance of human freedom and the limitations of government (morally and practically). It is generally better at managing resources and securing the conditions for the common good than the alternative economic models presently on offer to us. Like democracy, we have the responsibility to use it properly for the benefit of all.

P.W., August 2009

Dear Reader,

If you're reading this letter, you are probably one of the people that capitalism has benefited. So, to understand the need for change, you may need some Jesus-like ability to empathise with those for whom it has been a disaster. Even the economists, who have been the high priests of capitalism, are now confessing that the world's bottom billion have no chance of joining the rest of us if the present system continues. But what is your alternative?

The system as we have it now has gradually evolved through moments of business-inspired deregulation, most notably in the early '70s, '80s and '90s, both here and in the US. Therefore, what we need is campaigning for further gradual progressions in policy, in light of what we now know, to make markets fairer in service of the common good.

Crucially, the concept of the common good is missing from a system built on profits, and we lose track of how important that is for all of us.

Any wealth that someone builds is not just 'their own money', but has been accrued on the back of the 'common wealth' – their education, healthcare, transport, a legal system, the Internet, not to mention that of all their employees. That's why Jesus' proclamation to pay your taxes rings true for us. It's because we know it's not 'our money' at the end of the day. We are merely stewards. 'All the believers were one in heart and mind. No one claimed that any of his possessions was his own, but they shared everything they had (Acts 4:32). The early church made headlines because 'no one was in need'.

God's character, as expressed in the Old and New Testaments, is continually inclined towards those who are marginalised and forgotten. It has often been said that God has a bias towards the poor, and much serious theological work has been done to back up this statement. Even if you don't believe that as an *a priori* theological statement, however, the sad truth is, God *has* to have a bias towards the poor simply because we don't. In fact in general we have the exact opposite – a fawning deference towards the rich and powerful.

The last thirty years have seen an unprecedented increase in the gap between rich and poor, both in the UK and worldwide. While the capitalist system that has allowed this inequality to flourish is new, the injustices are not. As the prophet Amos testified, the poor are often forgotten because money equals power and influence. That's why many Christians are called to left-sided politics. They see an opportunity to 'speak up for those who cannot speak for themselves'.

We need laws because human nature sadly dances towards greed and accumulation rather than cooperation and sharing. The laws of the Old Testament were an exercise in practical theology. Land was handed back rather than allowing aristocracies to buy it all up. Fields were not ploughed to the edge, to allow the poor to eat. Debts were cancelled. There is never a discussion as to whether the recipients of this grace deserve it or not.

Unless you have a strange 'utopia is now' attitude to life, you know that we still need laws – relevant to our society – to allow it to run smoothly and fairly and to prevent an economic free-for-all. And, to God, these are as important in safeguarding community as other instructions regarding sexual ethics or murder.

The classic defence of capitalism is that 'a rising tide raises all boats', but the facts simply don't concur with this. The mantra of the kingpins of private equity was that their actions actually made the market more efficient for everyone, so we should excuse them the outrageous takings from deals where profit is the only bottom line. But to cling to this olive branch in the wake of the credit crunch is laughable. Their actions have led to the system grinding to a halt rather than becoming more efficient. And, who has been left to pick up the bill for their sins?

We believe that God became man in order to create a win/win situation, reaching out to those who didn't deserve it, not a story of winners and losers, and not a 'survival of the fittest' scenario. God involves us in his big story to redeem and reconcile all things to himself. This is a process of cooperation and not competition. This fundamental theological principle of cooperation, exemplified by the Trinity, is what left-sided politics at its best is about.

Nobody's perfect. And no one ideology is perfect. But you have to start somewhere.

A.F., August 2009

+

Some Questions You Might Want to Think about and Discuss with Others ...

1. Do you find one of these letters more persuasive than the other? Can you express why?

2. Is it possible that both of the above letters could be advocating economic systems that fit within the biblical moral vision, suggesting that it is how the system is implemented that matters, not the system itself? What might be the wider implications of your answer to this question?

3. How do you respond to the suggestion that God has a preferential option for the poor?

4. As a Christian, what do you think your responsibilities are in regard to your government's preferred economic policies?

5. What role do you think the Church has to play in free market economies? What underpins your conclusions?

part three

finding focus

distinctive

Stories make us who we are.

Without a story, we struggle to survive let alone thrive. We need to know who we are and where we belong.

A few years ago I spoke at a conference where a friend of mine – a community activist – was also taking part. During his seminar, he spoke of how, some years beforehand, he and his wife had adopted two children from South America. Their start in life had left them with deep emotional and psychological scars. He talked movingly about how his children needed a new family and fresh start. But much more than that, he said that what they needed most was a new story.

Through his work in nurturing communities, he had learnt that a story is a potent tool that has the power to do much more than simply recall information – it can drive transformation. Stories conjure with the possible. Stories hint at alternative visions of reality. Stories can create changed lives, even new worlds.

My friend spoke of the destructive story his children had inherited about who they were. Their story, he said, had come to control them. What they needed was an alternative. So, he explained how, with the help of what he referred to as a 'narrative therapy specialist', his two children were enabled to recognise that they, along with their adoptive parents, had a new story together – one which they could not only own, but live in. Armed with their new story, the remarkable thing was that his children were able to convert the painful memories of the past into a hope that brought transformation to the present and offered them a different future.

Our stories can trap us. But they can also set us free.

A story has the ability to direct our lives. We act and behave in accordance with it. We become who our story tells us we are. 'It is no accident that when they are asked to identify themselves most people recite a narrative or story,' commented psychologist, George Stroup.[63]

I recall talking to a street-gang member from a tough and deprived southwest London housing estate. 'Look at this place,' he said. 'How can you make this the basis of your life? In the end, if you do not escape, this becomes your story. You can't be more than this. You become your environment.'

A few months later, I sat in a prison room talking with a young man serving a sentence for murder. He had killed another teenager in a gang fight five years earlier but had benefited from half a decade to reflect on his crime. 'I was part of the wrong crowd,' he said. 'I'm not saying that any of them were any worse or better than me. We were all okay – it's just that we were bad for one another. Our problem was that we got caught up in something bigger than us.

'To begin with we'd just talk about being aggressive, as a way of protecting ourselves. But as time went by, when we saw others, we'd give them some mouth. Then one night someone turned up with a knife. Then I got one. We all got one. We were more than a gang. We were family. We had a shared code. An identity. A morality. We belonged together.

'Then, one Saturday night, we got in this fight – I even kind of liked the kid I stabbed; he was okay. It is just that, at that moment, it had to be him or me. And now I'm here. I am a murderer. A killer. That's me. This is who I am. This is my identity. This is my story.'

For better or worse, we all have stories that shape who we are and how we respond. More than that, the communities in which we live, and even our society as a whole, have dominant narratives that exert huge influence in determining what we believe about ourselves, the world in which we live and the way we should live in it.

These stories come from our families, our wider communities, science, our politicians, popular philosophy, the media, our religious beliefs and even our formal education. As they vie for our attention and commitment, they attempt to draw us into their spell. And once enthroned, they prove difficult to break free of. Their voices are persuasive and they whisper to us: 'You're ugly', 'You're nobody without the right label, badge or brand', 'If you don't carry a weapon you're not safe', 'Security is a big salary', 'You're too old', 'You're stupid' ...

Identity

When God appeared to Moses in the burning bush (Exodus 3:2), the Israelites were enslaved in Egypt. Whatever their heritage had once been, that story was now to a great extent being shaped by other factors. Israel's story was now one of oppression and servitude in which Egypt and its pharaoh held all the power. They were not free people but captives living in a foreign land.

Though they dreamed of liberation, things had been this way for four hundred years now, and there was little sign of hope on the horizon. Being slaves in Egypt, living under the backbreaking rule of Pharaoh and the power of the Egyptian gods was the dominant reality shaping Israel's story and, therefore, their identity, outlook and response to life.

So God began to lay down the foundations of a new story that would reframe their future, and he did so by giving Moses the core of a different narrative:

I have seen how my people are suffering as slaves in Egypt, and I have heard them beg for my help because of the way they are being mistreated.... I will bring my people out of Egypt into a country where there is good land, rich with milk and honey. (Exodus 3:7–8 CEV)

In effect, God was saying to them, 'I know your story, and it's one of horror and torment and oppression. And I see that you have come to understand yourselves only as oppressed and mistreated slaves. Nobodies. A forgotten underclass. But I see you differently. You will not be held captive much longer. You will be free. You are my people.'

Rather like the narrative therapist that helped my friend and his family overcome their destructive, life-shaping story, God was revealing to Moses and Israel a new story, which brought with it a fresh vision of who they were and what their destiny was. It was a story intended to transform not only Israel's future, but that of the whole world.

As we have already seen, centuries later, on a Galilean hillside, Jesus did much the same thing for a different group of people. 'You are the salt of the earth.... You are the light of the world,' he declared. His words were reframing reality for his audience – the downtrodden underclass of first-century Palestine: 'I know you've had your story told to you in a particular way, and that has shaped your idea of who you are, who God is and how you fit (or rather don't fit) into his plans and purposes. But I have come to tell you a new story. A better story. A transforming hope-filled story about who you really are and who you can become.'

Yahweh's message, which arises out of his character and spelt out so clearly by Jesus, is that our past, our failures, our sins, our enemies – none of these define us anymore. Neither are we determined by our economic situation, our social class, our education or our race. We are no longer victims of our previous track record or our circumstances. None of these determine our significance.

'Once you were not a people, but now you are the people of God; once you had not received mercy, but now you have received mercy' is the way that Peter puts it (1 Peter 2:10). Not only does that mean we are free, but more than that it means that we don't have to fight or struggle to prove ourselves, because the truth of who we are has already been established by Christ. 'Therefore, if anyone is in Christ, he is a new creation; the old has gone, the new has come!' (2 Corinthians 5:17).

How we think about and live out our lives with regard to issues as diverse as self-worth and motivation, wealth and poverty, anger and violence, the environment and climate change, consumerism and fair trade, abortion and euthanasia, sex and sexuality, war and peace and many more, is all determined by the dominant story that claims our allegiance.

But more than that, so are what we regard as the more mundane, though equally important, little attitudes and approaches we take, as well as the assumptions and decisions we make on a day-to-day basis, regarding our work, our money, our investments, our leisure time, our health and our relationships.

It is a big question. Whose story is shaping us? And has that story got the power to transform our lives, our communities, our society and the world in which we live for the better?

As we come to understand what it means that Jesus is Lord of the whole world, slowly we come to understand ourselves, our communities, our society and our world, more fully and truthfully. As Neil Messer puts it, 'You see the world, your own place in it and the way of life that is required of you differently once your identity has been shaped by this story.'[64]

None of this means that the memory of our past is lost, but rather it is transformed as God weaves it into his story of redemption. As Stanley Hauerwas and William H. Willimon observe in their book *Resident Aliens*, 'In Scripture, we see that God is taking the disconnected [and negative] elements of our lives and pulling them together into a coherent story that means something.'[65]

A New Perspective

Many of us grow up with the idea that right and wrong are determined by some form of universally accepted moral framework – a set of moral absolutes, or 'super-rules', that all cultures understand, sign up to and obey. A code that is inherently understood by all people, in all places and at all times.

In reality, ethical diversity is all around us. There is a huge difference between what the Church might regard as a set of Yahweh-ordained moral principles for the universe and a universally agreed set of moral principles.

Just listen to the conversation about politics and religion at a dinner party or down at the pub. It's very likely that some of our friends, family and work colleagues have very different and conflicting viewpoints on sex, the implementation of scientific advances, justice, education, war, the environment and so on. What's more, they will almost certainly believe they are right and everyone else is wrong!

The fact is, there never has been and never will be a universally agreed set of moral principles. It's meaningless to try to talk about ethics without first accepting that 'ethics' always needs qualifying – Kantian Ethics; Situation Ethics; Utilitarian Ethics; Jewish, Hindu, Islamic, Christian Ethics.

Whatever we may like to think, Christian ethics are not universal ethics – they are not just anyone's ethics. If they were, what would be so special about Jesus and our story? If the Church is just another source of conventional wisdom, a place to reiterate what everybody in society already knows, then what is different about Christ? Whatever we might say to the contrary, he becomes nothing more than a private motivation for what amounts to common sense.

If God does not exist, then the universe and human life take on one shape and – accepting that as fact – it is up to us to determine how our ethics work out from there.

But what if we dare to believe that this is God's universe, and he has revealed himself as he truly is through Jesus Christ? And what if, through that life sacrificed on the cross and by his subsequent resurrection, Jesus has defeated death and begun the work of the re-creation of all things? And what if one day this work will be completed as God finally wipes away every tear from every eye as his Kingdom becomes fully present? Daring to believe this will lead us to reach a very different conclusion about the moral framework in which we live, even though it may seem irrational to those who do not believe what we do.

At the very centre of this moral framework stands the cross. Therefore, the essence of our ethical approach is never superiority, but service. Being an apprentice of Christ is less about a label or status and more about the content of a life that is centred on sacrifice and peacemaking. As Paul explains in his letter to the Christians at Philippi:

> Your attitude should be the same as that of Christ Jesus: Who, being in very nature God, did not consider equality with God something to be grasped, but made himself nothing, taking the very nature of a servant, being made in human likeness. And being found in appearance as a man, he humbled himself and became obedient to death – even death on a cross! (Philippians 2:5–8)

Jesus is the king who conquers, not by violence, but by love. He does the very thing 'that kings cannot do and yet remain kings'[66] – he willingly surrenders his power. Alan Storkey puts it this way:

> In the Gospels, we are presented with a perspective on power so radical and disturbing that few have understood

or come to terms with it even today. For Jesus attacks the very notion of power as control over.... Human history is littered with castles, wars, slave trading, refugees, impoverishment, futile work, destruction, spy systems, bombing and other systems of effort which have resulted from the human need for control over.... Although we may focus on the worst examples, the acceptance of control over is ordinary in the lives of many people and states. But what if this idiom is a great human mistake? This unthinkable truth Jesus has presented to us.[67]

While it's true that the cross rejects the idea of power as 'control over', it's not a sign of our quiet, suffering submission to the philosophies that surround us. Rather, because of the resurrection, it marks our revolutionary participation in the ultimate victory of Christ over all other powers and worldviews. As Hauerwas and Willimon write: 'The cross is not a symbol for general human suffering and oppression.... The cross stands as God's (and our) eternal no to the powers of death, as well as God's eternal yes to humanity, God's remarkable determination not to leave us to our own devices.'[68]

There used to be a small denomination in the UK called the 'Peculiar People'. I remember seeing some of their few remaining buildings when I was a child. It seemed odd to me to call yourself 'peculiar' – and it probably wasn't the best marketing ploy, as perhaps their subsequent demise has proved. At a deeper level, however, they were right. To live by Christ's ethic, to be human, Christ's way (the way of the cross and the resurrection) means we are peculiar.

The story is told of a group of new police recruits attending their first day of training. The senior training officer welcomed them and then posed this scenario:

'You are on duty on a hot and busy day,' he said. 'You are nearing the end of your shift and are tired. As you stand on the crowded pavement talking with an elderly lady who has stopped to ask for directions, out of the corner of your eye, you spot a group of men running from a shop with a sales assistant in full chase shouting, "Stop. Thieves. Stop them."

'You excuse yourself as fast as you can and are just rushing across the street to intervene when, from down the road, you hear an awful crash. You spin round and there in the middle of the street are two cars that have hit each other, and a motionless motorcyclist lying on the ground next to his bike.

'Just as you are juggling with how to respond to this latest challenge you hear the cry of a child from above you, and, gazing up, you see the frightened face of young boy at the open window of a fourth floor apartment with smoke swirling around him.'

The training officer paused and then asked this question.

'In that situation, what would you do?'

There was a silence. Then one brave recruit raised his hand.

'Remove my uniform and merge with the crowd.'

To follow Jesus makes us distinctive. We don't have the option of removing the uniform. As the apostle Paul teaches: 'As God's chosen people, holy and dearly loved ... [we are to] clothe [ourselves] with compassion, kindness, humility, gentleness and patience. [To] bear with each other and forgive whatever grievances [we] may have against one another. Forgive as the Lord forgave.... And over all these virtues [we are to] put on love, which binds them all together in perfect unity' (Colossians 3:12 – 14).

In short, Paul is saying, 'You are God's people. Be distinctive, wear your uniform, clothe yourselves in Christ.' It is this distinctiveness (or peculiarity) that is essential to our faithfulness. The Church lives its life and models its responses based on something that most in our society dismiss or even scorn – the life, death and resurrection of a first-century Jewish rabbi from Nazareth, called Jesus.

The truth is, no ethic can be freed from the story that reveals, determines and sustains it, or from the people who imbibe it and so live it out. In other words, all ethical frameworks are what the scholars call 'tradition dependent'. As Stanley Hauerwas has noted:

All ethical reflection occurs relative to a particular time and place. Not only do ethical problems change from one time to the next, but the very nature and structure of ethics is determined by the particularities of a community's history and convictions.... The questions may look similar – What is good? What is evil? What is right? What is wrong? How should I respond? What should I do? Would it matter if ...? – but the answers to such things are determined not by a universally applicable set of ethical rules that stand over and against the lives of ordinary people and places, but are determined by the convictions, understanding, belief, culture, etc of the communities to whom such questions are asked.[69]

Morality, or more accurately our understanding of it, is relative to the norms of our culture. Whether an action is believed to be right or wrong depends on the moral norms of the society in which it is practiced.[70]

We might suppose that at least in the matter of taking life, all peoples would agree on condemnation. However, as anthropologist Ruth Benedict illustrates in *Patterns of Culture*, societies and communities differ widely in their moral practices.[71] For instance, in some cultures it has been held that it is the moral, god-given duty of the eldest male child to kill his parents after they reach a certain age, stemming from their belief that people are better off in the afterlife if they entered it while still physically active and vigorous!

In some cultures, the elderly and infirm are expected to sacrifice themselves in times of famine by leaving the community and facing certain death by starvation or exposure to the elements in order that the younger and stronger members can live on. By contrast, other cultures see the moral responsibility of the community as looking after every need of its elderly members.

Alasdair MacIntyre, a leading contemporary ethicist, says that moral frameworks must be grounded in a particular time and place and generated out of the communities in which they are to be practiced. He then goes on to explain that the contemplation and practice of these virtues becomes the soil which provides the cultural resources that allow that community to change and grow morally.[72]

In light of this, it should become clear that the depth and richness of the Church's distinctive story – created in the image of God, fallen, broken, called, forgiven, redeemed, tasked with the work of the Kingdom of God, recipients of the gift of God's Spirit, awaiting the renewal of all things and the return of the King – introduces us to ideas and a way of being that are completely outside of the understanding or comprehension of others. It is this that provides the soil from which our moral formation is possible. And once you understand all this, your way of seeing life is transformed.

Shine

Of course, in saying all this, it can't be denied that there will be some overlap, some points of commonality with the moral frameworks adopted by others. And this is so for at least three reasons:

First, all truth is God's truth. 'He makes the sun rise on both good and bad people. And he sends rain for the ones who do right and for the ones who do wrong' (Matthew 5:45 CEV). There is much that can be learned about the way the universe is from this observation. There are many experiences that we all share as humans: we have certain universal needs, and every one of us faces our mortality. All of which shapes common points in our understanding.

Second, historically our society has been steeped in the Christian tradition. Its beliefs and assumptions dominated society, influencing its politics and laws, shaping its values, its art and architecture, and holding the hearts of its people. And even though the memory of this is now fading fast, and we now live in what the social commentators call a 'post-Christendom' society, it still bears many of the marks of its theological, philosophical and moral heritage.[73] As Robert Jensen says, 'Western civilisation is still defined by Christianity, but as a civilisation that used to be Christian.'[74]

Finally, while it is true that what we believe shapes how we behave, we must still allow for our wickedness as well as our woodenness. The fact is, when it comes to walking the way of Christ, we are all at times stubborn and deliberately rebellious. Just as often, however, despite our best intentions, we simply miss or fall short of being like the Christ we are called to follow. Indeed, the most commonly employed term in the Bible that we translate as 'sin' (Hebrew *ht'*; Greek *hamart*) doesn't denote wilful rebellion or wrongful transgression; instead, it conveys the idea of missing the mark, rather like an archer trying but failing to hit a target. The assumption here is that though the intention of people is to try to hit the target, to be what God wants them to be, to be morally good and fully human, the simple problem is that, left to our own devises, we are just not up to it.[75]

We are not foolish enough, however, to believe that to choose to follow Christ as the basis for our lifestyle will make sense to others or that it will make our lives smoother or easier. After all, the Jew we base our ethics on was executed for his views and actions. But we do claim that we live this way, by this story, because it just happens to be true. It is the way that reality is. It is the way the universe is. It is the way that God is.

We can understand why other people, indeed, society as a whole, may disagree with us. Their disagreement is explained simply in the fact that they do not know or follow this crucified Jew from Nazareth. For Christian ethics can only make sense to those who are committed to Christ and what has happened through his life, teaching, death and resurrection.

But none of this means that Christian values or convictions are of significance only for the Church. Our claim is that it is only by learning to find our lives within the story of God that anyone can learn to see the world truthfully.

If the truth about God (as revealed in the Bible and chiefly through Christ) is true at all, it must be true universally – it is either the big story for everyone or no story for anyone! A Christ, without universal validity has no resemblance to the Jesus Christ that the New Testament claims him to be. 'Christ is Lord of all or not at all.' Or as it is stated elsewhere: 'Believing the Christian faith means believing that it is true and is therefore public truth, truth for all, truth which all people ought to accept because it is true.'[76]

Rather than retreating into its own privatised world in order to accommodate other voices, part of the Church's task is to recover the confidence that the gospel is not only 'a story' but 'the story'. To do this, we must also reject the limited vision of the Church as a place of private withdrawal from society. Our faith may be personal, but it can never be private.

We are called to do nothing less than live as a people whose ethic shines like a beacon to others, illuminating how life should be lived well. 'Christians ought not to hope for a society controlled by bishops or church synods.... It is through the presence and activity of committed and competent Christian men and women in the various areas of the common life of society that the Christian vision for society could become effective in practice.'[77]

God's story tells us that our lives are of value. The gospel is not just about God's act of forgiveness, it is also about his invitation to partnership. Filled with the Spirit of God, we are called to work to bring in the Kingdom. The Church is a revolutionary community with the goal of making disciples – disciples who transform the society they live in.

Or to put the same thing another way, it is said that William Booth, the founder of the Salvation Army, driven by his passion to see God's Kingdom come on earth in the here and now, ended his last ever public address, in London's Royal Albert Hall, on 9 May 1912, with these words:

While women weep, as they do now, I'll fight; while little children go hungry, as they do now, I'll fight; while men go to prison, in and out, in and out, as they do now, I'll fight; while there is a drunkard left, while there is a poor lost girl upon the streets, while there remains one dark soul without the light of God, I'll fight. I'll fight to the very end.

enlightened

'Okay. Let's do it. Let's play Who Wants to Be a Millionaire', announces Chris Tarrant at the beginning of the opening sequence of the film *About a Boy.*

'Who wrote the phrase, "No man is an island"? John Donne, John Milton, John F. Kennedy, Jon Bon Jovi?' he asks the contestant.

'Jon Bon Jovi. Too easy,' comments Will Freeman to himself as he watches the show on the TV and makes himself a coffee in his stylish bachelor apartment.

Will (played by Hugh Grant), who drives fast cars, enjoys casual relationships, and at thirty-eight, has rid himself of all responsibilities, adds that whoever did say 'no man is an island', it is absolute rubbish.

In my opinion all men are islands.

And, what's more, now is the time to be one. This is an island age.

A hundred years ago, for instance, you had to depend on other people. No one had TV, or CDs, or DVDs, or videos, or home espresso makers. As a matter of fact, they didn't have anything cool.

Whereas now, you see, you can make yourself a little island paradise. With the right supplies and, more impor-

section two | enlightened

tantly, the right attitude, you can be sun drenched, tropical,
a magnet for young Swedish tourists....
And I like to think that perhaps I'm that kind of island.[78]

Me, Myself, I

The Enlightenment is the term used to describe the movement that
began in the eighteenth century whose influence has played a huge
role in shaping so many aspects of our current Western philosophical ideas. One of the most important of these was that of the 'rational and isolated hero', who acts independently, who weighs, judges,
decides and acts, detached from his or her tradition, community,
family and history.

In this way, God was displaced from his role at the centre of thinking, and his place was taken by society's faith in the ability of human
reason to answer all our questions and solve all our problems.

This self-centred, individualistic approach to ethical life, the influence of which still pervades our society, was best articulated by the
famous eighteenth-century philosopher Immanuel Kant, a pioneer
of Enlightenment thinking, who declared, 'Have courage to use your
own reason. That is the motto of the Enlightenment.'

Our culture takes for granted the principle that any healthy society is
one where each person gets to be his or her own ultimate authority.
In fact, though unsaid, the common assumption is that society itself
exists primarily to assist the development of the individual and the
fulfilment of their needs and desires.

Indeed, our society insists that everyone is free to discover themselves and their own values, a belief expressed in the popular man-
tras we all learnt by heart: 'I'll do it my way', 'I'm my own boss' and
'You have no right to judge me'.

The individual is king and their freedom is paramount! 'Never in
human history has it been easier – indeed, almost mandatory – to do

one's own thing,'[79] comment Richard Koch and Chris Smith in their provocative book *Suicide of the West*.

But if our society has done away with God, it has not ceased to worship. Human beings have an insatiable desire to worship someone or something. Pete Lowman suggests that

> in each era since we turned away from the Bible's God, our culture has been shaped by one or more 'god-substitutes'.... They're the things that 'matter most' to us, the principles that dominate our lives, determining our sense of what's important and the sources we look to for truth and meaning, for the understanding of right and wrong.[80]

Everyone has become, or has invented, their own god – their own ultimate authority. If we no longer see ourselves as 'made in the image of God', and he ceases to provide our measure of life, our own ideas are all that we are left with.

Perhaps it was George Bernard Shaw who summed up the outcome of all this best when he defined hell as 'the place where you must do what you want to do'.

Belonging

In their book *Finding Our Way Again*, Brian McLaren recounts the story of Michael Polanyi, a Jewish chemist who lived and worked in Berlin at the Kaiser Wilhelm Institute of Science during the years leading up to the Second World War.[81] As Hitler's Third Reich became ever more powerful and extreme, however, Polanyi eventually fled Germany for England, narrowly escaping the ghettos and concentration camps where millions of his fellow Jews would be annihilated over the coming years.

The tragedy of the Holocaust changed Polanyi's life forever. But perhaps the deepest and most disturbing question for him – the one which consumed the rest of his life – was: How could the most advanced nation in the most advanced continent in the most advanced century in the history of history stoop to such barbarism?

Something was lacking in the West's single-minded pursuit of reason. What was it?

In search of an answer, Polanyi gave up his science lab and went to live and work among the ordinary tradesmen and women of his town. He became fascinated by the way they acquired, what he later came to call 'personal knowledge'[82] – the kind of wisdom and understanding that could only be gained by an apprentice working 'elbow to elbow' with a master craftsman. 'This "elbow" knowledge was qualitatively different from that promoted by the modern educational system of pre-war Germany,' suggests McLaren. 'That system had spawned plenty of graduates who could get straight A's in civil engineering, but it hadn't produced enough people who would refuse to use their skills to design the ovens of Dachau.'[83]

Without the ability for such discernment, Germany had become scientifically brilliant but morally bankrupt.

Polanyi's argument was that this moral bankruptcy was at least partly due to the progressive ideals of the Enlightenment, which, in many ways, Germany, and particularly Berlin, had been at the heart of. This had led to the belief that morality was discovered by individuals, through reason alone, and had slowly undermined that moral wisdom is held and passed on, generation after generation, through vibrant communities.

What Polanyi was coming to realise, and to argue, is that moral formation cannot be developed in isolation. Moral wisdom is practical wisdom and is dependent on community. It is impossible to live a virtuous life outside the context of a community. We have to belong in order to behave. Not only do we learn from the example of others, but our interaction with them corrects our responses. Simply reading manuals, or sitting in lecture theatres to learn, will get you nowhere.

You don't need to have a PhD in ethics in order to live well. Just as, rather ironically, having one is no guarantee of moral wisdom.

In their book *Resident Aliens*, Stanley Hauerwas and William H. Willimon, argue that we are not, as our culture has so often taught us, autonomous individuals with our own brand of morality that is unchallengeable. As they put it, moral wisdom 'is not something that comes naturally. It can only be learned ... by being in contact with others who are [also] disciples.'[84]

As I was writing this chapter, I found myself quite unexpectedly faced with a difficult moral decision, which, as I thought about it, would impact the life of another person (and perhaps many other people) in a profound and ongoing way.

Over the years, I have learned, albeit slowly, not to react and rush into instant decisions. I have learned from others, far wiser than I, to sit back, reflect and then respond, rather than to rush in prematurely, react and then regret! So, instead of acting on the first idea that came to me – as right as it seemed at that moment – I forced myself to pause, reflect, consider and pray. Then I made a phone call to a good friend who was also involved. We chatted together. She said some things that I hadn't thought of, and just wouldn't have seen by myself. We agreed to talk again the next day, by which time she had also sought out the advice of another close friend of ours who knew the situation. And together – in a way that none of us would have been capable of alone – I believe that we found truth; an honest but redemptive way of dealing with what otherwise would have been an extremely destructive situation.

Though we'd like to imagine that most ethical choices and decisions are simple yes-or-no, right-or-wrong scenarios, moral issues are far more complex than that, and this 'many-sidedness' means that the best responses hold these tensions in balance. The more compli-cated the situation we face, the greater our need to rely on discussion and dialogue with others about the dilemma. Only by careful exploration of the problem, aided by the insights and perspectives of others, can we hope to make good ethical choices.

Bonded

As human beings, we've been taught to prize our freedom above all other things. But to become a Christ-like person under our own steam is not just difficult, it is impossible. That's why, whenever the Bible makes statements like: 'Christ has set us free! This means we are really free' (Galatians 5:1 CEV), it quickly adds, 'Don't use your freedom as an excuse to do anything you want. Use it as an opportunity to serve each other with love.... Love others as much as you love yourself' (Galatians 5:13–14 CEV).

The people of Israel could never have imaged Yahweh dealing with them in ways other than the social and communal. The principle is no different for Christ's new community – the Church.

Real freedom is born, not from our insistence on our independence, but from community. Only this gives us true perspective. Only this enables us to know who we are and what our direction should be. Hard as it may be, and contrary to all our culture tells us, the first step to freedom is that of abandoning our autonomy. Together, but only together, we are able to develop and sustain a Christ-like way of being human.

If listened to, the lie of Enlightenment-style individualism cripples us, because as isolated individuals we simply lack the moral and ethical resources we need to be faithful disciples. It is only together, as the Church, that ordinary people like us are set free to achieve the extraordinary – to live beautifully. Therefore, the real question we should address is not how do I maintain my independence, but what sort of community do I need to be a part of to live the kind of life that will reflect God's character – a life of faithfulness, forgiveness, generosity and wisdom?

Every local church should be a countercultural community working to break free of the tyranny of the detachment and individualism in which our society is soaked. Renewal comes not from the wisdom and heroic actions of a few isolated 'super-thinkers', but rather through a community as it is shaped by the moral vision of the biblical story, as we seek to help each other live it out, day by day.

Probably, one of the most famous and certainly most quoted philosophical sayings of all time is the observation made by René Descartes: 'I think, therefore I am.' There is, however, a less well known, but perhaps far more honest proverb, the roots of which are not found in the rarefied academic atmosphere of pre-Enlightenment Europe, but in the harsh realities of the heartland of Africa: 'I am because you are; you are because we are. A person is a person through other people.'

As the former Archbishop of South Africa, Desmond Tutu once said, 'None of us come into the world fully formed. We would not know how to think, or walk, or speak, or behave as human beings unless we learned it from other human beings ... the solitary, isolated human being is a contradiction in terms.'

In a consumer environment, where the customer is never wrong, this means that the gospel brings about a head-on collision with many of our culture's most widely held values. We are all dependant on the churches to which we belong, to keep calling us back to the story of Yahweh, to keep speaking the truth to us, and to keep on raising the difficult questions – to keep re-firing our ethical imaginations – to help us to see life with different eyes.

I'll Do It My Way

It is to its own great cost that popular culture has bought so deeply into the 'I'll do it my way' philosophy of individualism. To the extent that our churches have swallowed that same kind of thinking, not only have they been weakened, but so has each one of us who claims to follow Christ.

Unfortunately, the way many people view their relationship with their local church today is as little more than a group of relative strangers with whom they meet on a weekly basis – to sing hymns and listen to a sermon – before heading off down their own separate pathway for another six days. Our experience of church is, therefore, reduced to a kind of self-help meeting designed to give those who attend a little bit of assistance on their way and to feel good about themselves – or at least better than they would have done otherwise.

So, rather than providing a counter to the individualism and consumerism of our society, the church ends up simply serving as another dimension of it, as it endorses the choices of its members and adherents, whatever they are.

Outside of the hot issues of sex and serious addiction to drugs or alcohol, how we choose to live is up to us. However big the car, however lavish and self-centred the lifestyle, however brash or brusque the manner – 'it is none of your business. It's my own life.' We don't want our rights and freedoms to be restricted. Instead, we want to be able to choose whatever course of action we feel is justifiable, however dubious the reasoning behind it.

Though we talk about 'making a commitment' to 'following the way of Jesus', in reality, we often choose to keep at least one foot in the camp whose motto is 'look after number one'. Hauerwas and Willimon say:

> What we call church is often a conspiracy of cordiality. Pastors learn to pacify rather than preach.... We say we do it out of 'love'. Usually, we do it as a means of keeping everyone as distant from everyone else as possible. You don't get into my life and I will not get into yours. This accounts for why, to many people, church becomes suffocatingly superficial. Everybody agrees to talk about everything superficial. Everybody agrees to talk about everything except what matters ... [because] 'This is none of your business. It's my own life,' and

so on. The loneliness and detachment of modern life, the way we are made strangers, infects the church too.[85]

One of the problems we face in so many of our churches is that of 'revolving door syndrome'. We have a big front door, but an equally big back door. We are successful at getting people into church, but too often we lose them just as quickly.

Recently, I talked to someone who had given up on church. I asked her why. She replied, 'Because I am so deeply disappointed with its superficiality.'

Huge numbers of those who 'try church' do so looking for something deeper than the loneliness, detachment and competitiveness of our wider society. They come looking for hope, for wisdom, for guidance – about their jobs, their ambitions, their fears, their problems, their relationships, their marriages, their children, their need for intimacy and their questions about sexuality.

It is vital that we supply them with something more substantial than a simple echo of their own thoughts. Our challenge is to invite them to join the adventure of following Jesus, to discover with us, a new way of being human – a way to live differently. For if we fail them, they will soon be gone, or, just as bad, spend the rest of their lives filling a pew somewhere but living disappointedly.

Confrontation

In Matthew 18:15–17 Jesus teaches his disciples:

> If your brother sins against you, go and show him his fault, just between the two of you. If he listens to you, you have won your brother over. But if he will not listen, take one or two others along, so that 'every matter may be established by the testimony of two or three witnesses.' If he refuses to listen to them, tell it to the church; and if he refuses to listen even to the church, treat him as you would a pagan or a tax collector.

The interesting thing is that Jesus doesn't suggest this approach as one of the options for those who might find it helpful. Instead, he mandates it. And to the extent that we ignore his words we weaken ourselves – and our churches. How do we grow morally without accountability? In what other way can we develop Christ-like responses and wisdom?

One of the biggest problems in our society is the lack of self-knowing. How many people do you know whose greatest weakness in life is that they are unaccountable? Nobody ever tells them what they really need to know about themselves (what everybody else already knows about them and often talks about together behind their backs!).

We have an urgent need to develop churches where honesty and gentle confrontation are valued. This implies both accountability and humility; the accountability to others that enables them to offer me honest feedback and guidance, and the humility that enables me both to recognise my weakness and to be open to their input. As Hauerwas and Willimon state:

> The indispensability of the church for Christian living is more than the practical observation that life is difficult and thus we need a little help from our friends. It is also a claim about how the church enables us to be moral in the first place. The church not only gives us the support we need in being moral, it also teaches us what being moral is.[86]

We need churches where we are known, accepted, nurtured and held to account, churches where honest confrontation is valued, even though we know it will sometimes be painful. It is ironic that real peace is only possible in a community that is strong enough not to shy away from such conflict. Jesus said, 'The truth will set you free' (John 8:32), but he didn't promise that it wouldn't hurt along the way sometimes.

For some of us who have a history within sections of the Church that have been marred by authoritarianism and the abuse of leadership, there is, of course, a natural fear here. But the answer to the problem of abuse is never that of disuse, but rather right use. To ignore our need for mutual accountability in the context of a committed Christ-centred community is to fall into the trap of isolation set by our culture's prevailing ill wind of individualism. Again, Hauerwas and Willimon write, 'Yet, what if our true selves are made from the materials of our communal life? ... By cutting back our attachments and commitments, the self shrinks rather than grows.'[87]

To understand just how important all this is, we need look no further than the story of Peter we find in the Gospels. The fact is, without Jesus – and the community of his fellow disciples – Peter might have been a good fisherman – perhaps he might have even become an outstanding one. But he would never have developed the courage and wisdom and faithfulness for which he is known. He would have never become half the person history remembers him as.

The Church believes in community. We believe that the individual thrives best within community and that truth is found together, in debate, in discussion, in lives shared. Therefore, the task of every church is that of the creation of people who are better than they would have been without the support of one another.

All this is why meeting together on a regular basis is so important for the Church. The spiritual and ethical battle is the one that we fight day to day, week in, week out. So we gather to sing our hymns, to worship together, to learn to see straight, to rehearse our values and to remind ourselves that we are called to be holy. We gather to remember who we are: the people of God, the followers of Jesus.

As the writer to the Hebrews puts it: 'We should keep on encouraging each other to be thoughtful and to do helpful things. Some people have got out of the habit of meeting for worship, but we must not do that' (Hebrews 10:24–25 CEV).

Churchless?

All this leads us to another huge question that has become a hot potato in our culture: Can you be a Christian without the Church?

If the sum total of salvation is nothing more than a one-off prayer, if being Christian is reduced to the right to wear a label or logo with little or no particular ethical content to our lives, then anyone can be a 'Christian' without the Church. But if following Christ is about the ongoing work of our redemption and moral formation, then the answer is an emphatic no.

In truth, the very question is simply another symptom of how deeply embroiled we are in exactly the kind of isolationist, individualistic philosophy that dominates our society. For those who choose to follow Christ rather than simply name-check him as their folk hero, the Church – the Christian community – is the primary ethical unit. Put simply, just as it was impossible for the first disciples of Christ to follow him in isolation – they had to do so in community – so today, things are just the same.

Even biblical interpretation is a community-based issue rather than the privatised 'thought-for-the-day' that we have so often turned it into. Scripture is too important to be relegated to occasional private study. Every book of the Bible, both the Old and New Testaments, is a communal text. The Old Testament emphasises that teaching was conducted by word-of-mouth in the context of a relationship. 'Tell your son.... Talk about them when you sit at home'.[88]

Among the early Christian churches, it was groups of believers, rather than individuals, who received the pastoral letters that we now know as the Epistles of the New Testament. And it was in the context of community that the Gospels were read and debated. None of the New Testament writers ever intended, or even imagined, that people would read their letters alone. When they were read, they were always read aloud in a group setting. Their content was thought about, debated, questioned, discussed, argued over and studied together. Conclusions about their meaning were reached as a collective. Individual insights and perspectives provided balance and alternative points of view.

A faithful church is a church that allows the Bible to breathe again in its native habitat. Indeed, our lack of robust, ongoing communal debate around the text of Scripture perhaps accounts, in part, for why so much of it is unknown or incomprehensible to so many Christians today. Every healthy church should be a big conversation around the Bible. Or to put it another way, all Christian ethics are social ethics – the Bible has no concept of the lone-ranger Christian.

Moral Mentors

As we have already discovered, in ancient times it was understood that ethical expertise was no easier to gain than expertise in any other area of life, that learning to be moral was just like learning any other skill.

But this means that mentoring is essential to the task of moral formation and development. There is nothing so helpful as an ethically inexperienced person having the opportunity to look over the shoulder of a morally mature and wise person.

In the Hebrew culture, in which much of the Bible was written, it was taken for granted that a person became just or merciful, faithful, self-controlled or caring by imitating mentors, teachers, family members and others from the community whose teaching and example modelled a character and lifestyle worth imitating.

So the rabbinic teaching method of Jesus' day consisted primarily not in attending lectures, reading texts and so mastering the material, but, instead, by focusing on the quality of the relationship between the rabbi and his apprentices as a means of getting to know and understand his way life. A rabbi's knowledge could only be taught from life to life.

'Jesus' [teaching was] ... not just about ideas,' comments education-alist, Charles Melchert and adds that

> education has been so associated with schools, books and ideas that we become misled – so we need to be reminded of apprentice-disciples and of learning from seeing others do things. If learning to love our enemies is an idea or theory, dismissal can come easily: 'Well, that's all fine in words or in theory, but it won't work in real life.' But when I see someone act it out in the real world ... or when I learn by trying it out myself, it is harder to dismiss.[89]

Whatever the skill, we know that training, coaching, ongoing advice and the support of wise and experienced fellow apprentices, along with hours of practice, repetition, debate and discussion, all held together by the discipline of being single-minded and resolute, are the ingredients of success.

Apprenticeship is as essential to the task of morality today as it was in Jesus' day. We learn good habits by watching people with good habits. So a person becomes just by imitating just persons. A person becomes compassionate by imitating compassionate people and the way they relate to the world.

Ancient Israel functioned as a predominantly oral society. The vast majority of communication was not via written texts, but through face-to-face relationships using the spoken word. As Melchert says,

> In a literate world, if I want words, I can find a book and read silently. An oral culture ... requires face-to-face presence in a way that a literate world does not.... We who are schooled in literate societies ... tend to forget that the bulk of what we know, especially what we know how to do in living our everyday lives ... [is also] learned and confirmed orally and

experientially, rather than from reading. Much of what we do daily continues to make use of orally acquired learning. We seldom look to ... literary productions to provide us with the know-how we need.... So we say, 'My mother always said ...', or 'As Grandpa often said ...', or 'My teacher said ...' Such learning is not only ... fruitful; it is a rich, holistic, embodied, sensory, and emotional experience that makes for lasting memories.[90]

And as through life we develop these disciplines and skills, so, in time, we will be called upon to play our role in mentoring others, both formally and informally. To the extent that the Church has come to believe that everyone's opinion is of equal value we have bought into the all-pervasive culture of modern individualism. Developing moral skill is as much about mentoring and apprenticeship as any other skill.

This is why the strongest churches are often multigenerational churches. A church comprised solely of twenty- and thirtysome-things will be impoverished and will run the risk of producing spiritual and ethical pigmies. One of our greatest strengths is capitalised when we bring generations of disciples together.

As Charles Melchert observes:

> We need to be reminded of apprentice-disciples and of learning from seeing others do things. If learning to love our enemies is an idea or theory, dismissal can come easily: 'Well, that's all fine in words or in theory, but it won't work in real life.' But when I see someone act it out in the real world (e.g., Gandhi, Dorothy Day, Martin Luther King Jr, Mother Teresa) or when I learn by trying it out myself, it is harder to dismiss.[91]

A good discipleship course is not a DVD with a glossy workbook. Discipleship is about much more than the elementary mastery of a series of doctrinal positions. Properly understood, discipleship must be about helping people to see with different eyes – about giving them the tools they need for the journey called life. Although books, videos and sermons may play a part in discipleship, they are always secondary to the main task of ensuring young Christians get the opportunity to look over the shoulders of older inspiring disciples of Christ as they both work at what it means to follow him.

There is no substitute for examples of Christian faith wrapped up in human form.

thinking christianly

So God created human beings in his own image,
in the image of God he created them;
male and female he created them.

GENESIS 1:27 TNIV

+

Homosexuality

For those of us who live in the largely tolerant and liberal societies typical of the developed nations of the West, it's politically and morally correct to see same-sex relationships as natural. Civil partnerships between people of the same gender have become an accepted part of our culture, and discrimination against someone because of sexual preference is against the law.

If the Christian community is known for having strong opinion on any ethical issue, however, then sexuality in general, and homosexuality specifically, must be it. Homosexuality has become the touchstone in the debate about the relevance of the Bible and the Church in our contemporary world. Indeed, such is the intensity of the dispute over the subject of whether homosexuality is in any way compatible with Christian faith that some denominations, particularly the Anglican Church, look like they may well implode because they are unable to find a way forward without an unlikely consensus.

Understanding what the Bible has to say on any important issue will always mean reading far more widely (and wisely) than one or two isolated passages. It will also mean a willingness to listen to those for whom a moral debate is more than simply an academic question. The following letters reflect something of the complexity and personal nature of discussing the Christian faith's view on homosexuality.

Dear Reader,

The Bible is clear that God's love is for all people, gay or straight, despite their sin. At the same time, however, it insists that God is a God of holiness, truth and righteousness. A biblical response to homosexuality must also recognise that there are factual distortions and ethical misunderstandings concerning homosexuality that need addressing. There are at least four common myths to challenge:

1. That homosexuality is inherited or genetically determined – there is no serious evidence for this.
2. That 10 percent of the population is homosexual. The actual figure for practising homosexuals is nearer 2 percent.
3. That homosexual orientation can't be changed. The existence of many people who have successfully resisted same-sex attraction and are living heterosexual lives demonstrates this.
4. That everyone who disagrees with homosexual practice is by definition 'homophobic'.

Most Christians who have seriously reflected on the matter believe that questions relating to same-sex attraction are part of a larger problem that has to do with issues involving sexual identity. A biblical response is not so much to homosexuality as such, but to the question of sexual conduct outside marriage, which according to Scripture is definitively between one man and one woman. No one is suggesting that experiencing feelings of same-sex attraction is a sin. But when carried out in practice, and when affirmed to be a normal variant of sexual behaviour, then it is deemed to be sin according to the Bible.

What does God really say in the Bible about homosexuality and does he say what Christians are saying? God's intention for human sexual activity is clear from the Bible. The division of humanity into two distinct but complementary sexes is not accidental but something good and planned by God when he created human beings.

God ordained that men and women should relate to each other sexually in marriage. There is a contemporary view that sexual relationships do not need to be heterosexual, exclusive or monogamous in order to be ethical, honest and loving. However, that view is not found in the Bible, which is unequivocal that the proper setting for sexual activity is marriage, that those who are not married should not engage in sexual intercourse and that those who engage in it should do so only with their husband or wife. In endorsing this, Jesus (referring to Genesis 1 and 2 as authoritative) said this was because a man and his wife 'become one flesh'.

The result of the above is that homosexual practice has been consistently condemned within the orthodox Christian tradition, not because of a few proof biblical texts, but because it falls short of a holistic Christian vision of human sexuality.

Of course, whether or not orthodox Christian tradition accurately reflects what God has said can be challenged. This is done regularly by questioning the classic biblical texts that condemn homosexual practice by suggesting, for example, that they have been wrongly or inconsistently interpreted or that the biblical writers were ignorant of the facts relating to homosexuality and that we know better today.

These arguments, however, do not hold water. First, the Bible always speaks negatively about homosexual practices and never commends homosexuality. Second, the texts in both Old and New Testaments are united in condemning all forms of homosexuality. Third, whilst the church now approaches slavery, contraception, divorce and remarriage and the role of women in leadership in ways that differ from historical practices, nevertheless, the church has not in these areas rejected Scripture but learned to understand it better. In the case of homosexuality, the church has not understood its reading of the Bible to require development because here, unlike the other examples, there is a consistent negative witness throughout the Bible. A major danger today is that claims of being led by the Spirit to change the teaching of the Bible can very easily disguise attempts to accommodate the Christian gospel to the spirit of the age. There is no authority given to human beings to change the plain truth of Scripture.

In conclusion, it is important in this debate that whilst the Bible must authoritatively shape Christian thinking about sexual relationships, the Bible must also shape our response to homosexual people by including and welcoming them as amongst those for whom Christ died.

D.H., August 2009

Dear Reader,

I remember vividly the day that our then thirty-one-year-old son 'came out' to us: how distressed he was and how hesitant when he said, 'I have something to tell you both. What I have to say is so disgusting [his word] that if you cannot cope with it, I will never mention it again ... I am homosexual.'

I remember his telling us how 'deceiving' us about his sexuality had become too great a burden to bear any longer; that he had not wanted to cause us any disappointment (grandchildren?); that he had feared rejection because, as Christians, we might support the Church's stance on the non-acceptability of homosexuality; how he had prayed to become heterosexual; how, believing himself to be 'flawed' sexually, he had sought to be perfect in every other area of his life and how that had caused such immense stress and anxiety that he had had to seek specialist help and face-to-face counselling. As he had been studying at university and working away for several years, he had endured all his anguish alone. We, his parents, had been unable to offer our love and affirmation when they were both most sorely needed. Shame, self-hatred, and fear of what might be the consequences of 'coming out' had kept him isolated from us.

Knowing nothing at that time either about homosexuality or about the Church's attitude or policy towards it, I was deeply shocked to learn that church teaching on the subject had been one of the main causes of my son's distress over the years. It could even have prevented us from ever knowing him fully.

In 2004, Desmond Tutu, former Archbishop of Cape Town, wrote in *The Times*, 'All over the world, lesbian, gay, bisexual and transgender people are persecuted. We treat them as pariahs and push them outside our communities. We make them doubt that they too are children of God – and this must be nearly the ultimate blasphemy. We blame them for what they are.'

Wise and thoughtful words from the pen of a gentle, compassionate and courageous man!

C.H., August 2009

+

Some questions you might want to think about and discuss with others ...

1. Do you find one of these letters more persuasive than the other? Why is that?

2. Whatever your view on the issue of homosexuality, where in the Bible do you turn to justify and substantiate your beliefs? Do you see any problems with your argument?

3. From a Christian perspective, heterosexuality, expressed in mutual, committed, loving, caring, faithful relationships, is recognised as something that reflects the nature and character of the God in whose image we are made. If that's true, can same-sex partnerships also reflect the character of God? What factors are shaping your thoughts and responses to this question?

4. How do you respond to the issues raised in the second letter?

5. Reread the quote from Desmond Tutu in the second letter. Do you agree with him? How do you respond to these criticisms if you don't agree with him?

part four

eyes wide open

countercultural

Do this in remembrance of me. (Luke 22:19)

These six words of Jesus have become a central part of the life of the worldwide Church.

Through the centuries, week by week, in obedience to Jesus' command, Christians have taken and eaten that morsel of bread and drunk, with thanksgiving, the wine.

But what if we've been missing Jesus' main point?

What if, when Jesus used these few words, he was referring to something beyond the constant re-enactment of this time-honoured ritual?

'What if,' asks Rob Bell and Don Golden, Jesus 'was talking about us actually enacting what the ritual is all about, over and over, again and again, year after year? What if the "this" he primarily meant wasn't the actual ritual he was leading his disciples through at that moment, what if the "this" was his whole way of life?'[92]

Some might be shocked by this interpretation. But it represents exactly the way in which we have traditionally understood the parallel story of Jesus washing the feet of his disciples – which in John's account of the Last Supper replaces that of the shared bread and wine – and the command to 'do as I have done for you' (John 13:15).

We have come to understand the bread and the wine we use in the Eucharist as 'sacraments' – defined by St Augustine as 'a visible sign of an invisible reality'. On the night before he died, Jesus broke the bread and offered the wine as symbols (or signs) of his life – a self-giving, servant-hearted life that was surrendered in love for others every single day, and that would soon find its ultimate expression through his sacrificial death (see Mark 10:45).

Perhaps then, when Jesus said, 'Do this in remembrance of me', what he really meant was, just like him, his followers are to be a sacrament – a visible sign of an invisible reality – for a watching world. Perhaps what he was saying should be heard as more than a command to share bread and wine, but understood as part of his call to sacrificial discipleship:

> Follow me! Act justly. Love mercy. Walk humbly with your God. Bring good news to a broken and suffering world. Announce freedom to captives. Feed the hungry. Provide water to the thirsty. Welcome the stranger. Clothe the naked. Care for the sick. Visit those who are imprisoned. Comfort those who grieve. Love your neighbour and love your enemies as you love yourself. Forgive as you have been forgiven. Live peacefully and patiently. Live gently and faithfully. Do these things, because then, you will have truly remembered me.

Babylon

Few people would dispute the fact that somehow, somewhere, our society has lost its way. Its imagination has been paralysed. Its sense of direction and vision has evaporated. It is devoid of a sense of journey, of adventure. It lacks belief in anything much more than its own self-expression and self-preservation. But without a compelling ethical vision, even as it loudly proclaims its freedom, in reality it finds itself stranded, directionless, impotent and marooned.

US General Omar N. Bradley was a brilliant soldier who played a strategic role in the successful American beach landings for the D-Day assaults and the progress of the allied forces as they pressed forward into occupied Europe. But he was no warmonger. He had seen the devastation of war, and knew what it meant. On Armistice Day 1948, he gave what was to become one of the most famous post – Second World War speeches:

> With the monstrous weapons we already have, humanity is in danger of being trapped in this world by its moral adolescence. Our knowledge of science has clearly outstripped our capacity to control it. We have many men and women of science; too few men and women of God. We have grasped the mystery of the atom and rejected the Sermon on the Mount. We are stumbling blindly through a spiritual darkness while toying with the precarious secrets of life and death.... Ours is a world of nuclear giants and ethical infants.[93]

If the gospel is true, the world needs the Church because, without it, the world will never regain a sense of vision, purpose or direction worth having. Or as the theologian Karl Barth put it, 'The Church exists ... to set up in the world a new sign which is radically dissimilar to [the world's] own manner and which contradicts it in a way which is full of promise.'[94]

The problem is that the world has changed. As James D. Berkley states: 'You may not have noticed or cared, since it has had so little effect recently, but that dubiously vain rooster called Christendom[95] – the organisational inbreeding of religion, culture and state – has gone the way of all flesh.... Make no mistake: the cultural phenomenon of Christendom is dead.'[96]

But this death is not a death to lament.

The loss of Christendom gives us the opportunity and freedom to proclaim the gospel in a way that is impossible if the main social task of the Church is to serve as just another helpful prop for the state. But it also presents us with the challenge of doing the hard work of wrestling with what it means to live out the revolution of an authentic biblical morality in an alien culture and context.

As Bishop Graham Cray has observed, 'All the major Church traditions in [the West] have been shaped by Christendom – by an expectation that they have a special right to be heard and that people "ought" to listen to them.... But we are now one voice among many.'[97]

What does it mean to be distinctively Christian in the strange world of post-Christendom, where many people don't even know that they don't believe because they still live with the assumption that you are 'Christian' simply because of the place of your birth or your nationality?

Many theologians draw a direct parallel between the experience of exile for the Old Testament Jewish people in the city of Babylon and our current post-Christendom situation, where we can still *remember* the social dominance that the Christian faith used to enjoy, but we no longer *experience*. Says theologian Kenneth Leech, 'As Christians enter the twenty-first century, they do so as exiles, strangers and pilgrims, aliens in a strange land. They will need to learn the strategies of survival, and to sing the songs of Zion in the midst of Babylon.'[98]

The Jews in the Exile were well acquainted with what it meant to live in a strange land, aliens trying to stake out a living on someone else's turf.

Before being exiled, living in Zion (Jerusalem), they enjoyed a city where Yahweh was publicly honoured and worshipped. Where the Temple and the palace worked together. Where their faith was enshrined in national life. Where the people around them shared their values. Where the stories taught to their children were the stories they knew and loved. Where the public festivals and celebrations gave them the opportunity to express their personal faith.

Put simply: they felt at home.

But Babylon was different. Here, in exile, Yahweh was not even known, let alone honoured or worshipped. Here there was no temple. Here they were forced to work out their faith without the support of the institution. Here the people around them had very different values to their own. Here the stories being taught to their children were unfamiliar and worrying. Here the public festivals and celebrations were difficult, forcing them to choose between their faith in Yahweh and that expressed by the society around them.

Put simply: they were a long way from home, and they felt it.

This historical backdrop informed the New Testament writers and led to the idea that in this world, Christians are 'resident aliens'.[99]

The writer to the Hebrews (11:13) talks about those who follow Christ being 'strangers on earth', whilst 1 Peter 1:1 and 2:11 both speak of Christians as 'strangers in the world'. And in Philippians 3:20, Paul writes 'our citizenship is in heaven', which the James Moffatt Bible more vividly translates as 'we are a colony of heaven.'

This powerful idea is taken up by the English word *parish* – which is derived from the Greek term *paroikos*, meaning 'stranger's house' – and presents the local church as a 'colony' of resident aliens in a particular community. We are called to be both *resident* and *alien*, at home and not at home, in the culture that surrounds us.

The experience of exile – potentially disastrous for the faith, identity and even existence of the Hebrew people – ultimately became one of renewal. Their witness is that it is not only possible to sustain a robust faith, but to develop new depths of moral integrity through such an experience.

Likewise, there are ways in which we, as the twenty-first-century Church, cannot only respond, but grow through our 'exile' experience, so that it becomes an equally rich time of discovery, creativity, innovation and growth.

Learning in Exile

David Smith suggests that in the twenty-first century, two equal and opposite dangers face the 'church in exile', just as they did the people of Israel in Babylon.[100]

The first is *insular traditionalism*, or *isolation*, where Christians choose to protect themselves by battening down the hatches and keeping their distance from the culture around them. The result of this approach is that the sphere of activity is shifted from 'without' to 'within', from society to the individual soul and 'internal church work'.

Though, very occasionally, the isolationist church might dare to venture out, as David Bebbington explains, even when it does so, it lacks confidence and tends to be overly defensive.

> [This] style of engagement with the ills of society has encountered a number of risks. One has been [that] ... a belligerent tone, an inflated rhetoric and exaggerated charges have often marked the campaigns.... Apart from tactical considerations, there is the problem that a hectoring tone is a poor advertisement for Christianity. A militant moralism rarely reflects the meekness, the kindness and the longsuffering reflected in Scripture. Few aspects of evangelical religion have done more to deter converts than the stridency of the popular campaigns it has mounted.[101]

The second danger for the church in exile is *cultural assimilation*, or *accommodation*. What once seemed like a strange and alien culture to us, slowly comes to feel like 'home', as our surroundings subtly corrupt and co-opt us. This is, of course, particularly true of the 'next generation' – those who never experienced the journey from Jerusalem to Babylon.

The assimilated church easily confuses what is successful with what is faithful. It is readily seduced into the kind of activism that, if probed, is largely built on the presumption that God is superfluous to the new situation. Its tactics, strategies and planning are, therefore, based, not so much on faith in God, but unbelief, and an over reliance on process instead.

As Stanley Hauerwas and William Willimon explain,

> As it goes about building bigger and better congregations (church administration), confirming people's self-esteem (worship), enabling people to adjust to their anxieties brought on by their materialism (pastoral care) and making Christ a worthy subject for poetic reflection (preaching) it slips further and further into the place where God really does not matter.[102]

For the assimilated church, being 'in the world' and serving it, is never the problem. In fact, its greatest problem is that it is all too willing to serve the world. It becomes 'nothing more than the court chaplain, presiding over ceremonies of the culture, a pleasing fixture for rites of passage, like weddings and funerals, yet rites in which our presence becomes more and more absurd because we are saying nothing that others do not already know'.[103]

The assimilated church ends up as nothing more than the dull exponent of socially acceptable political ideas with a vaguely religious tint. In a Western democracy, politicians of all shades and philosophies will always be keen to pat us on the back and offer us seats at their table in return for our loyalty to, and support of, their campaigns and policies. The assimilated church is a very helpful prop to the state as its gospel is subtlety adapted and domesticated to fit society's values.[104]

But our mission in life is not to run errands for the government or for wider society. We march to the beat of a different drum. The Church is here to serve the Kingdom of God. Sometimes this will make us popular, sometimes unpopular – but we do not exist to be chartered by the government. Though we may work with government – just as Daniel and his friends, Shadrach, Meshach and Abednego did in the

Babylonian exile of the Jewish people – our calling is neither to serve the political left or right. We serve Christ. Our task is to assert that God, not governments, rule the world. Our difference is to be his difference.

Rather than *isolation* or *assimilation*, the church in exile is called to walk the pathway of *distinctiveness* (or, put slightly differently, genuine *holiness*), where Christians engage the culture they find themselves in with a confidence born out of their belief that God is the God of the whole earth. As Ajith Fernando explains, 'By their life and witness, they challenge the ... [prevailing culture] ... when it opposes God's wisdom, and they demonstrate that God's way is indeed the best way.'[105]

The *distinctive* church has no interest in withdrawing from the world. Equally, it is not surprised when its witness evokes hostility, and even suffering, from the world in which it is placed. Its main task is simply to be faithful to Christ in all things.

The distinctive church seeks 'to influence the world by being the church, that is, by being something the world is not and can never be, lacking the gift of faith and vision, which is ours in Christ. The confessing church seeks to be the visible church, a place, clearly visible to the world, in which people are faithful to their promises, love their enemies, tell the truth, honour the poor, suffer for righteousness and thereby testify to the amazing community-creating power of God.'[106]

As the people of God learned in exile, 'Whatever power the kings of Babylon display, God's power is greater. However big might be their empire, God's Kingdom is bigger. However unshakable their dominion might appear, it is as nothing compared to the dominion of God.'[107]

Or as Jesus made clear when he stood in front of Pilate: 'You would have no power over me if it were not given to you from above" (John 19:11).

In the shadow of the growing power of Hitler's Third Reich, the leaders of what was to become known as Germany's 'Confessing Church' met together at the end of May 1934 in the city of Barmen.

There they issued the historic Barmen Declaration, mostly drafted by Karl Barth, with input from others, including Dietrich Bonhoeffer and Martin Niemöller. Niemöller was later to preach a sermon entitled 'Christ Is My Fuehrer', for which Hitler would eventually have him arrested and imprisoned in the notorious Dachau concentration camp, from which he was only released by the Allies in 1945.[108]

The Barmen Declaration was written in direct opposition to the acceptance of the Nazi regime by the majority of the Church in Germany, represented by what was known as the 'Faith Movement of the German Christians'.

The problem was that even under the threat of Hitler's regime, many German theologians were unwilling to shift from the tenets of traditional Lutheranism, which includes what is known as the 'Doctrine of the Two Kingdoms'.[109]

Martin Luther's views had originally been developed to address another issue, in another context, in another era, over four hundred years beforehand. But for those who couldn't play Jazz, who only knew the rulebook approach, they were interpreted as implying that matters of state were exclusively matters of state and not the business of the Church, and vice versa.

And perhaps it was a combination of this inflexible 'stick to the letter of the law' approach to their ethics, combined with the fear of losing their seat at the chancellors table, that silenced their voice.

In response the Barmen Declaration – a prophetic condemnation of Hitler's totalitarian rule – specifically rejected the subordination of the Church to the state. Christ, it declared, cannot be co-opted by, used in the service of or be remade in the image of religious or political ideologies created by fallen structures in opposition to God. And with the same clarity, it asserted that Christ alone is the one Word of God – the source of all authority and truth – whom we must hear, trust and obey.

Even today, the Barmen Declaration and the distinctive engagement of Germany's Confessing Church speaks to the whole Church in every place of 'exile'.

Iconic

An icon (Greek *eikôn*, meaning 'image') is a religious work of art, most commonly a painting, from Eastern Orthodox Christianity. More broadly, however, the term is now used in a wide number of contexts for any symbol or likeness that signifies or represents something bigger than itself.

Last year I visited the island of Cyprus. While there, I had the privilege of spending a couple of hours in an old Byzantine monastery in the foothills of the Troodos Mountains. An elderly Orthodox priest explained to me that one of the historical reasons that icons of Christ were so often adorned with gold was that when housed at the heart of a building, with little natural light, they would pick up and reflect whatever illumination there might be so that the image of Christ would become the most obvious, attractive and eye-catching item in the monastery.

This is the way we should think of ourselves as Christ's Church within the world: icons that reflect Christ. We are called together, to play the role of a living, walking, talking icon of the invisible God.

'The Church's most important moral contribution to the society around it is not a distinctive and countercultural moral argument, but a [distinctive] and countercultural way of life that witnesses to the new possibilities opened up by following Jesus Christ,' said Neil Messer.[110]

The most credible form of witness (and the most 'effective' thing the Church can do for the world) is the actual creation of a living, breathing, visible community of faith. The only way for the world to know that it is being redeemed is for the Church to point to the Redeemer by being a redeemed people.

Of course, this is exactly the reason that many people say they don't believe in God. They look at the Church and say that they cannot see anyone within it who looks much different from somebody who does not believe.

Part of the problem may be that these onlookers have too limited an idea of God, which prevents their seeing him at work in the lives of ordinary people. But it is just as likely that sometimes we have failed to demonstrate the character of God, or to be different in the way that God is different.

Though our social involvement is not motivated by the false hope that through political action alone the world will be changed, neither do we accept the view that no change is possible. Instead, our task is to engage, because through our actions, and the power of God at work in us, real change is possible.

A few years ago, as part of our ongoing youth work, our church in London launched a radio station (with a license to transmit on FM for four weeks through the summer), which gave local teenagers the opportunity to broadcast to their community. Our church building – where the studio was based – is situated in the heart of an area with serious crime issues, including violent knife and gun crime.

The whole project proved to be a huge success, with several hundred young people from the local area choosing to get involved. At the end of our four week run, we asked the local police station if they could tell us if there had been any measurable impact on crime levels amongst young people in the area.

We knew that we would have made some kind of difference. But what we were not prepared for was their answer: youth crime in the area for the month of August – the month that we broadcast for – had not just gone down. It had stopped!

A few months later, I was visited by a government officer who wanted to talk more about our experience. We sat in the coffee shop we run in our church building and talked. He told me that, in government terms, we had run what he called a very successful 'CRI' (Crime Reduction Initiative) and asked me whether we would like some funding to deliver a twelve-week project as a follow-up.

I took him over to buy another coffee. On the side of the coffee bar is an old brass plaque, which used to stand in the pulpit of the previous church building. It simply reads: 'This pulpit was first preached in on June 8th 1783.' I showed it to the government official and explained that our church had served as an effective 'CRI', non-stop, for over 220 years. The radio station was just one small part of that ongoing role.

Probably the only way of measuring the overall impact of our church on its wider community would be to shut it down for a very long period of time until the last residual of the influence of its 'salting' effect has completely disappeared. It is a local icon. Together, the wonderful team of committed people who make it up reveal the face of God to our local community. And as they see his differentness, they too are slowly but surely transformed.

'If you have seen me, you have seen the Father,' claimed Jesus. Our task is to look and act like Jesus, so that we are able to say, 'If you have seen us – if you have seen our church, our community of Christians – then you have seen Jesus.'

The Church doesn't have a social strategy, the Church is a social strategy. Our story is our morality! Churches are communities that create countercultural people – shaped by, and living out, a different story. Our task is to tell the story, to live in the story, to live the ethic, to be the ethic.

Living It Out

If the term *ethics* took a holiday, we would best replace it simply by talking about 'being human'. Our ethics are our way of seeing, our way of thinking, our way of responding and relating, our way of being. And it is the outworking of these built-in habits, instincts and practices that should determine the creative, inventive and positive ways we find to respond to the big moral issues as well.

Recently, a young woman wrote this letter to me:

> Dear Steve,
>
> Having been brought up in a Christian home, I always believed abortion was wrong, that was until I found out that I was pregnant.
>
> Fear, panic and guilt gripped me. How would I tell my parents? What about my university place? I could not cope, and so I made the most painful decision of my life, to seek an abortion. After all, it wasn't really a baby, only a cluster of cells and it was my body and no one else's.
>
> Yet, if this was true, why was I walking around Mothercare in a daze and refusing to eat certain cheeses?
>
> They talk about a 'right to choose', but my abortion was arranged and rushed through within a week. I felt as if I had no choice.
>
> After the abortion I could not stop crying. I lost interest in school, it didn't seem important any more. And I felt so bad all the time. Then I found this website all about abortion and the help you can get. And I started to talk with someone, well online really, to start with. I did this course called The Journey. That was last year. And somehow it helped me face what I had done and I was able to forgive myself. I even wrote a secret letter to my little baby, to say sorry.
>
> No, I don't believe in abortion. I have learnt that to God my baby's life was very precious. God 'created my baby's inmost

being in his image, made in the secret place.... His eyes saw my baby's unformed body' (Jeremiah 1:5; Psalm 139:13 – 16). The Bible screams life from beginning to end. I love the story when Mary visited her cousin Elizabeth and her baby leapt in her womb because he recognised the Son of God at only two or so days old.

In this country, I am staggered that one in three women will opt for an abortion. How many of them are women like me, in crisis, rushed into decisions without the support they feel they need to cope or choose? If only they were cared for, they might find that way out and realise that they did not really want to lose their baby. It is such a painful time.

Surely Christians should be affirming the importance of the life of both the mother and the unborn child. I read a shocking passage the other day. Jeremiah said that the death of a baby is a direct attack on God's very nature (Jeremiah 7:30 – 31 The Message).

It seems to me the most dangerous place for a child is in the mother's womb. When will we wake up and show God's love and grace as well as his truth?

Yours sincerely,

The primary way that most of us have been conditioned to think about big issues, such as abortion, is to devise a 'Christian' position and then to lobby government as hard as we can to support it, with the goal of seeing it enshrined in law.[111]

And, of course, the more 'muscle' we can demonstrate, the bigger and better resourced, financed and connected we are, the further we hope to get.

It is only because we are fortunate enough to live in a developed, modern democracy, however, that Christians in our society can (just like every other pressure group in town) push for the legislative embodiment of our point of view in the first place. This, of course, has not been the case historically for much of the Church, for most of the time.

There are, in fact, no biblical passages that explicitly deal with the subject of abortion as such. There is no specific 'rule' to cover it.[112]

Though the issue of abortion is never directly addressed in the Old or New Testaments, it soon became of very real concern to the early Church leaders, mostly because of the culture of the Greco-Roman world that Christianity began to enter as it grew. What's more, as all the historical documents from the earliest centuries of Church history show us, the Church developed an unambiguous approach to the subject. For instance:

> 'You shall not murder a child by abortion nor kill one who has been born' (the Didache, A.D. 80–140, 1.377).[113]
> 'Abortion is killing human life that is under God's care, design and providence.' (Clement of Alexandria, Paedagogus, A.D. 190–200).
> 'In our case, murder is once for all forbidden. Therefore, we may not destroy even the foetus in the womb.... To hinder a birth is merely a speedier way to kill a human. It does not matter whether you take away a life that has been born or destroy one that is not yet born' (Tertullian, A.D. 197, 3.26).

It is also an important but little-known fact that abortion was illegal throughout the Roman Empire. A woman who aborted her child could face long-term exile, and the person who provided her with the poison for the abortion (the vast majority of abortions at this time were induced by poisonous drinks) could be sentenced to slave labour for life.

But the Church's 'pro-life' stance was very different, and far more creative, than that adopted by the society around it.

Instead of condemning them for their sins, there is much evidence to show that the early churches provided places of refuge for pregnant women in desperate situations, where they would find acceptance and support as well as the medical care they desperately required and an alternative to the abortion of their child.

More than that, not only did the churches provide for the physical needs of mothers, they also ran orphanages for children born of unwanted pregnancies. In fact, it is perhaps no coincidence that some of the early Church's greatest leaders started life as orphans.

Even after an abortion had taken place, the churches were there to offer the woman involved the housing, alongside the medical care and spiritual support that she so desperately needed.

In our generation, rather than be known for a self-righteous, point-the-finger kind of attitude towards teenage pregnancy, and the high rate of abortion in our society, perhaps our response would be far more in line with God's character if we adopted practices similar to that of the early Church.

What if the Church was first known, both locally and nationally, for giving its time and money to create shelter, support and care for young women, so often trapped by their lack of real options and love?

The harsh reality is that 'whenever Christians think that we can support our ethic by simply pressuring [government] to pass laws or to spend tax money, we fail to do justice to the radically communal quality of Christian ethics. In fact, much of what passes for Christian social concern today, of the left or of the right, is the social concern of a church that seems to have despaired of being the church.'[114]

The result is, the gospel becomes diluted. Often, without even recognizing it, our tendency is to water down our ethical positions, not on the basis of what is faithful to God's character, but rather how far we think we can push government to comply with our demands without losing our seat at the table.

So, we end up arguing about issues like how late in a pregnancy an abortion can take place, and whether we approve of the morning-after pill being sold over the counter to teenagers, rather than demonstrating a radical commitment to providing alternative realities for the women and children involved.

The primary political solution Christians have to offer our troubled society is not new laws or advice to government – although we may well, from time to time, find ourselves involved in both. The most creative social strategy we have to offer is the Church. Here we can demonstrate to society a way of being that it can never hope to achieve through social coercion or governmental action.

No clever language or arguments can substitute for the necessity of the Church to be a community of people who embody our language about God. Our churches are our theology. Any and every Christian ethical position is only made credible by the action of the Church.

As Christians, we understand the principle well. In the words of James, 'Faith that doesn't lead us to do good deeds is all alone and dead!' (James 2:17 CEV). Or to put it slightly differently: Virtue without action is nothing.

adventurous

'What would Jesus do?'

This instantly recognisable phrase first became popular in North America back at the end of the nineteenth century, following the publication in 1896 of Charles Sheldon's book *In His Steps*, which was subtitled *What Would Jesus Do?*[115]

But over the last few years, it has made a resurgence, as witnessed by the craze in some circles for bracelets, badges and bookmarks, all bearing the famous inscription 'WWJD?' – an abbreviated form of the same question.

Though some critics have dismissed the WWJD? initiative as nothing more than a tasteless exercise in consumerism, in truth, it serves as a kind of daily 'litmus test' for countless thousands of Christians who use it as a reminder that it is Jesus' moral example, which they seek to follow day by day.

The obvious problem, however, is that though it is always entirely appropriate to ask 'What Would Jesus Do?' it is often very difficult, if not impossible, to construct any kind of answer to this question based entirely, or sometimes even primarily, on the evidence of 'What Did Jesus Do?'

Firstly, the Gospels only cover a limited amount of material, as they acknowledge themselves (see John 21:25). More than that, no matter how many new rules and regulations the Church constructs, in a sense we are only ever dealing with yesterday's world, rather than the challenges of today.

Secondly, Jesus did not live in a world where he was confronted with many of the kind of moral issues and choices we find ourselves faced with today. As the German poet and philosopher Gotthold Lessing famously expressed it, we have to look at the life, death and resurrection of Jesus across the 'ugly wide ditch' of history.[116] So:

Would Jesus be for or against stem cell research?
Would Jesus be for or against birth control?
Would Jesus serve as a chaplain to the armed forces?
Would Jesus negotiate with terrorists?
Would Jesus speak at the local mosque if invited?
Would Jesus join a multifaith discussion group?
Would Jesus join a trade union or strike for more pay?
Would Jesus drive a car, and if so, which one?
Would Jesus drink beer, stick with red wine or re-evaluate and go tee-total?
Would Jesus buy a home, just rent or live in a commune?
Would Jesus get private health insurance or use the NHS?
Would Jesus vote? Who for? Why?
Would Jesus take vacations? Abroad? By plane?
Would Jesus offset his carbon footprint?
Would Jesus turn off his phone in a prayer meeting?
Would Jesus take a view on homosexuality?
Would Jesus complain about media misrepresentation?
Would Jesus turn the other cheek if mugged on the street?
Would Jesus train as a clergyman – if so for which denomination?

The honest answer to many of our contemporary WWJD? questions, is simply this: He didn't! None of this is to imply that it is harder to walk the way of Christ today than it has ever been. It is just that it is different!

The ability to respond to life, to the moral and ethical problems we face in a Christ-like way, can't be supported simply by trying to patch together a WWJD? handbook for every situation, made up of texts extracted from the Gospels about WDJD? (What *did* Jesus do?)! Answering the WWJD? question asks more of us than this.

Indeed, the sooner that we grasp that Jesus' intention was never to give his audience a definitive ethical manual on right and wrong, the healthier and more morally competent we will become.

Jesus came not to provide us with an exhaustive 'moral A-to-Z', but rather to train us to see. Not to imprison us in a moral straightjacket, but to equip us with a vision of what we might become. He came to set us free, to give us the resources to live beautifully.

For instance, at the end of his parable of the good Samaritan, when Jesus tells the expert on the law to, 'Go and do likewise' (Luke 10:37), he was not expecting him to tuck it away in his head so that, if he ever faced an identical situation to the one in the story, he would know what to do. Rather, Jesus was trying to get him – and us – to see, via the parable, the bigger moral vision of the Kingdom of God on earth. In this way, the lawyer would be able to creatively apply to his own life the principles and habits it encouraged, wherever life led him.

Likewise, when Jesus announced, 'If any of you want to be my followers ... you must take up your cross each day and follow me' (Luke 9:23 CEV) was he really implying that each of his hearers should aim to follow an identical pathway to his through life? Of course not. What he was doing was suggesting that they adopt the same habits and attitudes – those of service and sacrifice – that he demonstrated on a daily basis, because in doing so, they would have the tools to do the right thing in any given situation.

Rather than a complete encyclopaedia of moral responses to cover every conceivable situation his followers could ever face, Jesus' moral teaching compromised mostly of short sketches, mere examples of the thousands of imaginative, fresh and effective ways in which their character could be shaped with the goal of imitating their Father in heaven.

For all this, however, many people still fear that if you give up on living by rules and regulations you are, in effect, giving up on the discipline of the Christian life. And as soon as you do that, they warn, 'you are on a slippery slope into woolly liberalism'. In truth, however, as we have seen, the formation of moral habits and practices is a real and ongoing communal discipline. Whereas blind obedience to a set of inflexible rules is not only a lazy and poor substitute for moral formation, it will also stunt your moral growth.

Journey

One of the great tragedies of life is that so many movements that start with a dynamic and organic vision end with a sterile code.

In reality, of course, those who claim to hold set moral positions on all things deceive only themselves. How many Christians do you know whose attitude to the use of Sunday or other faiths or private health care or divorce and remarriage or sexuality or women in leadership or the environment, has changed, or been nuanced, across the years?

Over the centuries, and still today, Christians have had different and changing attitudes and moral stances to issues such as war, nuclear armament, capital punishment, race, slavery, the ownership of guns, government, dress codes, alcohol, entertainment, money, ownership … the list is endless. As Pope John Paul II is quoted as commenting,

'It is not that the gospel has changed, it is just that our understanding of it is slowly growing.'

N. T. Wright tells the story of a theological student in Kenya who listened intently to a lecture given by a European professor about the search for the historical Jesus. Bemused and frustrated, the student suddenly burst in to the flow of the lecture, 'If the West has lost Jesus, that is their problem. We have not lost him. We know him. We love him. We don't need to search for him.'[117]

As Wright goes on to remark, however, as appealing as this kind of bold certainty might at first appear, it is, in fact, a big mistake. To assume that we have got Jesus 'pinned down', 'sussed out' or 'summed up' is not simply arrogant, it is foolish. Our lifelong task is to ceaselessly and relentlessly pursue Jesus.

'Follow me!' With that short and simple challenge, Jesus invited ordinary people to become part of a lifelong, world-shaping adventure, a journey that would surprise them with each new turn of the road.

In order to know Jesus, we have to follow Jesus. It is at one and the same time a simple yet profound invitation.

In fact, in a very real sense, we have to follow Jesus before we can ever know him, for we can only discover him in relationship. Engaging with Jesus, as the misconceptions of his original disciples demonstrate, is essential to understanding him. But, furthermore, it is also true that we have to know Jesus before we can know ourselves. 'How can we know the truth of ourselves as sinful and misunderstanding, but redeemed and empowered, without our first being shown, as it was shown to his first disciples?'[118]

Salvation is an adventurous journey, but we are empowered morally as we embark on this adventure together. As Paul tells the church in Philippi: 'My dear friends ... continue to work out your salvation with fear and trembling, for it is God who works in you to will and to act according to his good purpose' (Philippians 2:12–13).

We are a people on the move, just like Jesus' first disciples, breathlessly trying to keep up with him. And this adventure will present us with many unknowns, internal arguments over which turn to take in the road, conversations and debates along the way, introductions and farewells, much reflection and looking back, as well as anticipation of the terrain still ahead.

Up Close

I listened to a professional photographer talking about his life and work on a radio programme. His story was fascinating. Much of his career had been spent in volatile and dangerous situations around the world, capturing pictures to be syndicated for use by the international press. Some of the most famous images we have from war-torn regions and natural disaster zones, and interestingly, also of dangerous wildlife, have come from his camera.

Towards the end of the programme, the interviewer asked, 'What is the essence – the magic ingredient – of a great photograph?' I still remember the answer, word for word: 'There are obviously a number of technicalities that are important, but in my business, the key to real success is simply this – get close. If your pictures aren't good enough, it is because you are not close enough.'

"Without Christ – not one step. With him – anywhere," said David Livingstone.

In the words of William Spohn, Jesus' 'call is to "follow me", not to follow a set of concepts, a code of conduct, or an institution.'[119]

We follow Jesus, not a set of nebulous and undefined concepts such as compassion or love. Nor is our task to bring compassion or love. Instead, our task is to fulfil Christ's challenge to bring in the Kingdom of God, which implies and defines a very specific understanding of compassion, love and, for that matter, every other virtue.

The hope of the world is not to be found in a set of disembodied and generalised principles, it is discovered in Jesus and through communities centred around his story, which bring context, meaning and reality to the principles we articulate. Bill Hybels says,

> Authentic Christianity is not learning a set of doctrines.... It is a walk, a supernatural walk with a living, dynamic, communicating God. Thus the heart and soul of the Christian life is learning to hear God's voice and developing the courage to do what he tells us to do.[120]

Which is one reason why not everyone joins in. By choosing to live within a tight set of rules and inflexible regulations, it is all too possible to talk things up and exude an air of certainty about where you are and where you are headed, even though secretly you suspect that you are lost. It takes a great deal more courage to step out from life's rigid framework and venture with Christ into the unknown.

As Paul later explains when he writes to the Christian community in Rome: 'Do not conform any longer to the pattern of this world, but be transformed by the renewing of your mind. Then you will be able to test and approve what God's will is – his good, pleasing and perfect will' (Romans 12:2).

In other words, it is as through the discipline of following Christ *together*, and developing habits and practices that echo his, that our thinking is transformed and, as a community, we discern God's will.

As inescapably individual as all discipleship is – it is, as we have seen, also always essentially collective. All discipleship is communal. As Proverbs puts it: 'As iron sharpens iron, so one man sharpens another' (Proverbs 27:17).

Moral wisdom is the outcome of learning to think and act consistently in a manner that is shaped by the example of Christ, the community of the Church and the leading of God's Spirit. Only this can provide us with the discernment to know God's will, even in the most difficult of circumstances and amid the pains and pressures of twenty-first-century life.

Blind Spots

The TV studio was hot. The debate was equally heated and passionate. The panel was comprised of politicians, academics and various religious leaders. The discussion was about religious fundamentalism and oppression, abuse and violence.

'What you are failing to accept,' stated a well-known church leader, addressing an Imam rather accusingly, 'is that Islam, in it's most fundamental and radical forms, devalues women. It denies them the same educational opportunities as men. It marginalises their role and contribution to society. And it oppresses them and undermines their rights and freedoms as women by insisting on prescribed dress codes, which are an outward symbol of entrenched and outmoded attitudes.'

The Imam sat and listened intently, if a little uncomfortably, allowing the full list of accusations and concerns to be put to him, and the subsequent applause from the audience to die down. Then he stood to respond: 'As you rightly suggest there are certain aspects of some interpretations of Islam that many people in Western societies find morally repugnant and that they feel undermine what they believe to be the freedoms and rights of women. This I recognise and accept. But here is what puzzles me.

'As I walked to the studio this evening, my senses were assaulted by advertising billboards on the roadside and by posters on buses and shop window displays. Many were using young women, sometimes in provocative, seminaked poses, to try to "sell" a lifestyle. And I know that what you call family entertainment – your films and TV – do the same. Forgive me, but I also know that your church grouping – your denomination – does not grant leadership to women.

'Tell me, what am I to understand about the morals of Western society from this? What value do you place on women? What is their role and contribution to society? It makes me want to ask the question, Which culture is really doing the oppressing?'

It is perfectly possible to be a Christian and yet to think in 'sub-Christ-like' or even 'anti-Christ-like' ways. As Jesus put it bluntly to his disciple Peter, 'Away with you, Satan. You think as men think, not as God thinks' (Matthew 16:23 NEB).

It is wise to remember that even our best thinking and behaviour is never fully, finally Christian, but only ever more-or-less Christian than it was previously. Whenever we forget this, instead of Christ judging our ideas, his name ends up being used to justify our behaviours – including, unfortunately, both our ancient and modern crusades.

The End

As the saying goes, everyone loves a happy ending.

But by 'ending', of course, we don't actually mean 'end'. What we really mean is 'outcome'.

We all enjoy stories that have a good outcome, or resolution. Indeed, some Hollywood film companies make hundreds of millions of dollars each year by supplying us with a continuous diet of exactly that.

And what we enjoy in a story, we also long for personally. We dream of the 'goal' or 'outcome' towards which our lives are moving – a great job, a successful career, a life-long partner, loyal friends, a comfortable home, financial security, good health, maybe even fame and fortune, and a long and happy retirement – in short, to feel good about ourselves and life.

Ethicist Alasdair MacIntyre suggests that we should think of our lives as a story (which he calls a 'narrative unity'), governed by a *telos*. *Telos* – a Greek word – literally means 'end' or 'completion'.

MacIntyre goes on to explain that no ethical system is intelligible or motivational if it is not 'teleological', that is, if it does not include an account of the *telos*, purpose or meaning of life.

Jonathan Wilson, in his book *Gospel Virtues*, says that the question for any community or culture is always 'how we get from where we are to where we should be'. Therefore, our overall purpose (*telos*) determines our morality (our way of living and being human), which becomes the means to accomplish our task.[121]

In other words, we will always struggle to find a sense of moral direction until we have some indication of where it is that we are headed.

If your life was a story, what would it be about? What would be its most important themes? What would be its subplots? Which bits of it could you leave out?

Only after having decided what their story is about, is any individual or community in a position to identify their *telos*, or goal. Once their goal is decided upon, it becomes much clearer which habits and practices they should and shouldn't adopt and develop.

So, for instance, how do you decide whether to go out with your friend tonight or stay in and prepare for tomorrow's meeting? You think about the story of your life. What's more important to the story of your life, seeing your friend or the preparing for tomorrow? You can only make these choices – which are all moral decisions – if your life has a *telos*.

From ancient times, it has been held that the *telos* of life is what the scholars have termed *eudaimonia*, a classical Greek word that is commonly translated as 'happiness', though it more accurately means 'human flourishing' or 'well-being'.

But the followers of Jesus see things with different eyes, because for us the story of his life and teaching, death and resurrection is definitive to our understanding of the *telos*, or 'end' of all life. And though human flourishing is central to this story rather than the 'end' itself, it is simply one facet of an altogether greater vision – that of the in-breaking Kingdom of God.

The biblical narrative couldn't be clearer. As William Spohn has said, 'Jesus does not come teaching timeless truths or moral principles but proclaiming a radically new initiative ... the resurgent reign of God.'[122]

Each of Jesus' choices was centred on this one goal. As Jesus summed it up himself:

> *The Spirit of the Lord is on me, because he has anointed me to preach good news to the poor. He has sent me to proclaim freedom for the prisoners and recovery of sight for the blind, to release the oppressed, to proclaim the year of the Lord's favour. (Luke 4:18–19)*

Jesus' objective was never self-promotion or self-aggrandisement but instead the establishing of the Kingdom of God. And it was this vision that informed his day-to-day responses.

So it was that his message and life were what the scholars would call thoroughly eschatological – about the 'end' of the world – where the *telos* is not about an apocalyptic destruction of everything that exists, but the fulfilment of God's purpose.

> *'This, then, is how you should pray:*
> *Our Father in heaven, hallowed be your name,*
> *your kingdom come, your will be done on earth as it is in*
> *   heaven.' (Matthew 6:8–10)*

The invitation is to join in with this unfolding story – the story of God. Salvation is not primarily about 'my story' but '*the* story'. Our personal stories are always secondary – we place ourselves in God's history. The adventure of redemption is that of joining in with, and playing a part in, the redemption of the universe – a new heaven and a transformed earth!

It is clear from Jesus' life and teaching that the Kingdom of God is, at one and the same time both present and future, or both 'now and not yet'. Though through Jesus' life and work it was already breaking in, its ultimate but sure fulfilment was still future.

Because of this, our ethics – our way of being – does not begin with anxious questions of what we ought to do to make things right. God has put and is putting things right. Rather, they begin with God's invitation to us to live as citizens of his Kingdom and to work in partnership with him, where the new world he is creating is taking visible and practical form.

Empowered by God's Spirit, we are active moral agents in the world as we work to bring in the Kingdom of God on earth as it is in heaven. Or to put it theologically, our ethics, our values, should all be eschatological choices.[123]

The *telos* of a local church is, therefore, not to provide great services and a good feeling in the congregation – though, of course, there is nothing wrong with great services and good feelings. However, the overall goal of a Christ-centred life and community is in the final analysis not necessarily to 'feel good' but to 'know good' and to 'do good'. For rather than feathering our own nests, our purpose is to serve as part of the kernel of the in-breaking coming Kingdom.[124]

In the words of the vision contained in Revelation 21:

> *Then I saw a new heaven and a new earth, for the first heaven and the first earth had passed away, and there was no longer any sea. I saw the Holy City, the new Jerusalem, coming down out of heaven from God, prepared as a bride beautifully dressed for her husband. And I heard a loud voice from the throne saying, 'Now the dwelling of God is with men, and he will live with them. They will be his people, and God himself will be with them and be their God. He will wipe every tear from their eyes. There will be no more death or mourning or crying or pain, for the old order of things has passed away.'*

> *He who was seated on the throne said, 'I am making every-*
> *thing new!' Then he said, 'Write this down, for these words are*
> *trustworthy and true.' (Revelation 21:1–5)*

The Church's cry is: if the future looks like this, let's work to bring it here, now!

One Sunday morning a few months ago, our church in Waterloo, London, was exploring exactly this theme – the 'now and not-yet nature' of the Kingdom of God. Dave, who was preaching that day, first read the famous passage from Revelation 21 and then, in the context of our mission, 'translated' it, helping us see our community with different eyes:

> It was 8 o'clock on Monday morning.
> I was standing by Lambeth North station.
> And I saw a new London coming down from the heavens.
> I saw a teenager leaping out of bed with joy, laughing with the freshness of the morning.
> I saw elderly ladies skipping down Kennington Road.
> I saw children paddling in the River Thames.
> I saw a football match in Kennington Park and the teams were mixed people from every people group: asylum seekers and taxi drivers, policemen and prisoners, pensioners and politicians. People from every race and class playing and laughing in the sun.
> I saw a street party where the people were eating and dancing because there was hope again.
>
> ⸻
>
> And I looked across the community of South London; a community of hope, a community of grace, a community of warmth.
> And, in the clearness of the morning, I looked down into the Elephant & Castle and there was no more asthma, no more

unwanted pregnancies, no more debt, no more violence, no more overcrowding and nobody was too busy.

The River Thames was flowing with crystal-clear water.
There were no more needles and condoms in the park.
No more sorrow of family breakdown.
No more poverty.
No more need.
No more unemployment or mind-numbing jobs.
No more hopelessness.
No more sadness and tears, only joy and laughter.
No more discrimination.
No more drunken clubbing. No threats, no fears.

The dividing walls were gone.
Families and neighbours were restored.
There was no more rubbish, no dealers, no guns, no knives, no dangerous dogs.
There were no racial tensions, just one harmonious mix in Technicolour.

And I looked and I saw kids playing football in the streets, and neighbours cheering them on.
I saw homes without locks on the doors, where a welcome was always guaranteed.
I saw a playground with climbing frames that weren't rusty, where children threw themselves in the air without fear of harm, where the teenagers helped the little ones up to the highest climbs.

I saw a London where neighbours shared favours and returned them without pressure or obligation.

I saw a London where hearts were unbroken, partnerships are lasting, peaceful and happy.

I saw a London where families eat and play together.

I saw a London where tears were wiped away.[125]

Now that's a vision worth living beautifully for!

thinking christianly

I know, LORD, that we humans are not in control of our own lives.

JEREMIAH 10:23 CEV

+

Euthanasia and Assisted Dying

In our contemporary world, euthanasia – and, therefore, the issue of assisted dying – is a hot ethical debate – a real headline-grabber.

As things stand, but for a handful of exceptions, euthanasia is illegal around the world. There is increasing pressure on our politicians, however, to open the way for euthanasia as an option for those who find the sufferings of this life unbearable when faced with terminal illness or degenerative disease. Indeed, while this book was in production, Debbie Purdy – who suffers with multiple sclerosis – won a landmark court case in the UK to have the law clarified whether someone who assists a loved one to die (commit euthanasia) can be prosecuted. She wanted reassurance that, were her husband to travel with her abroad and assist her in dying, he would not be charged with manslaughter or assisting manslaughter on his return home. She went on to describe the ruling in her favour as a 'right to live, not a right to die', as she says she can now wait longer before making a decision about when to end her life.

Most statements on this issue by the Christian community indicate a concern over the possibility of further legalisation, which might legalise the practice of euthanasia. Many

Christians believe that the premature ending of life (whether assisted by another or not) flies in the face of the Bible's teaching about the sanctity of human life and the right of God to determine when it should end.

It is, however, a complex issue, and the following letters, both written by Christians, represent two very different points of view (though not the only points of view!) on how our understanding of God might inform our response, both now and in the future.

Dear Reader,

The media claims that the majority of people in the UK want to change the law to allow physician-assisted suicide. Presumably those people also think that any opposing view illustrates a callous disregard for those who are suffering.

But what are we really talking about here?

We are talking about a doctor prescribing a lethal dose of medication knowing that it will kill, something illegal in Britain. Those who argue for a change in the law talk about the ending of suffering, dying with dignity, a person's right to choose.

When one is faced with one's own suffering or that of a loved one, these issues are painful and difficult, yet for a Christian, and indeed the rest of society, surely a change in the law would be a step too far. By definition, to legalise euthanasia means that a judgement is being made about the value and quality of the life of another individual. This is not academic; we are talking about real people.

As Christians, we are called to care. By allowing a person to end their own life, we are in fact opening the way for the vulnerable in our society to be threatened. When will a right to die become a duty to die? Who dare make the judgement that the quality of life a person with learning difficulties has is not worth anything? Many families, even though the road is hard, would disagree. Who says that an elderly person is not worth saving because they are old? There could be a huge pressure on them not to be a burden to their family.

All the major world faiths oppose euthanasia, and as Christians we need to be hearing what God is saying to us. Whilst it is true that apart from the apparent ending of King Saul's life at his own request by an Amalekite soldier in 1 Samuel 31, the Bible does not specifically mention euthanasia, what it does tell us is that we are all made in God's image (Genesis 1:26–27). Therefore, the life of every human being is uniquely precious, and as such, it must be given dignity and honour from conception until its natural end. We also know that human life is God's gift to us (Acts 17:25); this means we are not the owners, but rather are the stewards of it. The psalmist declares that 'my times are in your hands' (Psalm 31:15). There are also clear prohibitions against the deliberate taking of innocent human life (Exodus 20:13).

The prophets remind us that a just God demands that we care for the needy and vulnerable. Although not always easy, surely the truly compassionate response to demands for assisted dying lies in good medical treatment meeting a patient's physical, social, psychological and spiritual needs. Those of us who have sat with a dying relative or friend whose pain has been controlled know how important it is to finish well having run the race (2 Timothy 4:7).

As Dame Cecily Saunders, the founder of the Hospice Movement, put it, 'We will do all we can not only to help you die peacefully, but also to live until you die.'

N.L. August 2009

Dear Reader,

Euthanasia (the act, or practice of killing incurably sick or injured individuals, or assisting them to die, for reasons of mercy) is one of those issues that really gets to the heart of how we, as the Christian community, handle ethical decision making.

Naturally, one of the biggest problems we face is that the Bible does not address euthanasia – certainly not as we define it for the purpose of ethical and legislative decision making. There are, of course, the Old Testament commands not to take another person's life – though the subsequent bloodshed (sometimes directed by God) makes it difficult to know how we are to read such imperatives.

Being more positive, it is clear that life is a precious gift, given by God. Therefore, it is argued, it must be valued at all costs. That said, perhaps our attention should be towards the giver rather than the gift.

So, for example, some wish to argue that we must oppose euthanasia, even for those people who are clearly suffering and close to death, on the grounds that we are 'playing God'. But surely we must weigh this against those commands, actions and teachings of Scripture that paint God as one who is loving, caring, kind, compassionate, merciful and understanding – and the call on his people to be the same.

Barring miracles (and miracles are, by definition, not normal expectation, even for those of faith) the majority who seek euthanasia are terminally ill and have little time left – a time that may well be one of suffering (physically, emotionally and spiritually), not only for themselves, but also for those who love and care for them.

Clinging to a life that is so obviously ending in suffering seems counterintuitive to the fundamental Christian hope that this 'life' is not all there is and that death is not an end but a beginning – where there will be no more suffering, crying or pain (Revelation 21). Indeed, do we not console ourselves that the departed are 'at peace now' and 'their suffering ended'? It seems paradoxical, therefore, that we preach a suffering-free eternal life, and yet, at the same time, argue that life must be clung to doggedly until no more breath can be squeezed from our mortal bodies, however tortured our lives have become.

For Christians, euthanasia – and, therefore, the service of assisting a person to die – shouldn't be seen as autonomous self-determination – a usurping of God's right to take life away. Rather, it should be a decision made in faith, by a caring and compassionate community. Indeed, to leave individuals to make such decisions alone would be an act of the greatest abandonment, and most certainly contrary to the moral character of anyone wishing to call themselves a follower of Jesus.

We are not taking a life. We are allowing a person the right to willingly give it up, and to trust the God who has given them that life that nothing can 'separate us from the love of Christ … even suffering or death' (Romans 8:35 ff).

If one does not fear death but cannot any longer bear the suffering and pain of this life, then euthanasia can be seen as an act of loving compassion and mercy that reflects the character of the God who gives life – and the only one who can sustain it after death. What's more, given the opportunity, dying can and should be a deeply spiritual time, a chance to consider one's life and prepare for something much deeper and profound.

Nothing is inevitable, but it certainly looks like the future will be one where euthanasia becomes acceptable, if not legal, within our society. Which means that the Christian community (who have such a hope-filled message about life and death) need to consider the ramifications of refusing to support others in transitioning their lives from this life into the next. After all, a statement of faith or a theological position will not dissuade people of genuine Christian faith from asking the Christian community to assist them in dying – and that is where the truest test of our faith begins.

A.M. August 2009

+

Some Questions You Might Want to Think about and Discuss with Others

1. How do you deal with fact that the Bible doesn't say anything directly about the contemporary issue we label 'euthanasia'?

2. What problems do you see with the arguments, both for and against euthanasia?

3. Do you think the commands not to take another person's life apply to those who are terminally ill and suffering? Why?

4. If it is possible to interfere with 'natural processes' by lengthening life, why should it not be permissible to shorten life as well? It is often said we are 'playing God' when we end life prematurely, but are we not doing the same if we extend life beyond what otherwise would be its natural end?

5. Does euthanasia make a judgement about the value of life?

6. Why would a loving, merciful, compassionate God not want us to end a person's suffering by euthanasia?

7. As a Christian, do you want the right to have a say when you die? What factors underpin your answer?

acknowledgements

Our thanks goes to all the following who, in different but equally important ways, have helped us to write this book. Wendy Beech-Ward, Pete Broadbent, Graeme Bunn, Cornelia Chalke, Ruth Dearnley, Judith Doel, Andy Flannagan, Christine Holt, Don Horrocks, Krish Kandiah, Nola Leach, Jeff Lucas, Ian Macdowell, Bob Mayo, Sue Robbins, Russell Rook, Kay Surry, Paul Swinn, Jeremy Thomson, Ruth Valerio and Paul Woolley,

Steve Chalke and Alan Mann, October 2009

notes

1. As John Drane notes: 'In Canaan itself, the Ras Shamara texts depict El as the father of the gods and head of the pantheon at Ugarit [an ancient cosmopolitan port city, sited on the Mediterranean coast]'; in John Drane, *Introducing the Old Testament* (Minneapolis: Fortress Press, 2001), 226.

2. YHWH is known as the *Tetragrammaton* (Greek, meaning 'word with four letters'). YHWH was written with four consonants only; ancient Hebrew had no written vowels – or even vowel points. These were added much later, by which time pronouncing the name of God had already been forbidden for generations. One of the theories is that Jewish people stopped saying the 'Name' out of fear of violating the Third Commandment: "You shall not take the name of [YHWH] your God in vain" (Exodus 20:7 NKJV). Still today, when the term is read out loud by Jews, it is universally substituted with the word Adonai, Elohim, Hashem or Elokim, depending on circumstances. According to rabbinic tradition, however, YHWH continued to be pronounced by the high priest on Yom Kippur (the Day of Atonement), the only day when the Holy of Holies of the Temple would be entered. Still, with the destruction of the Second Temple in the year A.D. 70, this use also vanished and the original pronunciation was totally lost.

3. Michael Goheen and Craig Bartholomew, *The Drama of Scripture: Finding Our Place in the Biblical Story* (Grand Rapids, Mich.: Baker/Brazos, 2004), 41.

4. 'The Great Hymn to the Aten' and 'Two Hymns to the Sun God', in Miriam Lichtheim, *Ancient Egyptian Literature, Volume 2, The New Kingdom* (Berkeley, Calif.: University of California Press, 2006), 86–88 and 96ff.

5. Thorkild Jacobsen, 'Hymn to Enlil', *The Harps That Once ...: Sumerian Poetry in Translation* (New Haven, Conn.: Yale University, 1997), 108ff.

6. Terrence Fretheim, 'Yahweh', in *New International Dictionary of Old Testament Theology and Exegesis*, vol. 4 (Grand Rapids, Mich.: Zondervan, 1997), 1296.

7. Walter Brueggemann, *Theology of the Old Testament* (Minneapolis: Fortress, 2005), 158.

8. Though the Bible says nothing of Abram's early life, there is an ancient rabbinic legend (contained in the Book of Jubilees – a Midrashic commentary on Genesis and part of Exodus) which is also found in the Qur'an (Q 6:75–79), that his father Terah, was an idol maker in Ur. At an early age, Abram began to question the authenticity

of these idols, and later, as a young man, not only confronted his father about this but deliberately broke them all – except one – calling his community to monotheism and the worship the one true God. As a result Abram found himself condemned by King Nimrod of Babylon and cast into a furnace, which, however, miraculously failed to burn him.

Whether or not this story is true, in Genesis 12 not only does Yahweh reveal himself to Abram as the one God of the whole world who will bless not only Israel, but all peoples of the earth, but Abram chooses to venture out on the journey of a lifetime with this God and, in doing so, becomes the father of monotheism.

9. Brueggemann, *Theology of the Old Testament*, 177.

10. Drane, *Introducing the Old Testament*, 214.

11. The Ten Commandments are also repeated later, in Deuteronomy 5:6–21.

12. Andrew Sloane, *At Home in a Strange Land: Using the Old Testament in Christian Ethics* (Peabody, Mass.: Hendrickson, 2008), 170.

13. Ibid.

14. The Mishnah, meaning 'repetition', is one of the most important works of rabbinic Judaism and the first major redaction, or edit, into written form of Jewish Oral Torah or Law. The Mishnah does not claim to be the development of new laws, just a collection of existing oral laws, traditions and folk wisdom. It was compiled from the teachings of the rabbis between A.D. 70 and A.D. 200 by the group of rabbinic sages known as the Tannaim. The period during which the Mishnah was assembled spanned about 170 years, and five generations. Tradition claims that the first full edition of the Mishnah was edited around A.D. 200 by Rabbi Judah ha-Nasi when, according to the Talmud, the persecution of the Jews and the passage of time raised the possibility that the details of the oral traditions would be forgotten. Before the Mishnah, Jewish scholarship was predominantly oral. Rabbis expounded on and debated the Tanakh, the Hebrew Bible, without the benefit of written works (other than the biblical books themselves). The oral traditions were far from uniform and varied among various schools, the most famous of which were the House of Shammai and the House of Hillel. Judaism holds that the Oral Torah was received by Moses at Mount Sinai in parallel with the Five Books of Moses, the (written) Torah, or what we know as the Pentateuch, and that these together have always been the basis of Jewish Law. The Oral Torah is believed to be the exposition – or interpretation – of the Written Law as relayed down through the years by the religious leaders of each generation. It is not scriptural, but is regarded as authoritative in practical terms. Thus, Jewish law and custom is based not only on a literal reading of the Torah, or the rest of the Tanakh, but on the combined oral and written traditions. In fact, as the Mishnah was studied extensively over the centuries, rabbis added commentaries to its contents. The written combination of Mishnah and this commentary is known as Talmud. Rabbis in Jerusalem produced their Talmud by A.D. 400, while Babylonian rabbis brought together their more extensive version around a hundred years later. It is this Babylonian version that is now generally referred to as the Talmud.

15. John Rogerson, 'The Old Testament and Christian Ethics' in Robin Gill, *The Cambridge Companion to Christian Ethic*s (New York: Cambridge University, 2001), 30.

16. Taken from *The West Wing*, season 2, episode 3, 'The Midterms', Warner Bros. Television.

17. Stanley Hauerwas and William H. Willimon, *Resident Aliens: Life in the Christian Colony* (Nashville: Augsburg, 1989), 54.

18. *Blackadder*, season 2, episode 5, 'Beer' (1986) by Richard Curtis and Ben Elton.

19. Gerald Hawthorne, 'Holy, Holiness', in Ralph P. Martin and Peter H. Davids, *The Dictionary of the Later New Testament and Its Developments* (Downers Grove, Ill.: InterVarsity, 1997), 486.

20. Drane, *Introducing the Old Testament*, 295.

21. Hawthorne, 'Holy, Holiness', *Dictionary of the Later New Testament*, 485.

22. 'The Egyptians were cruel to the people of Israel and forced them to make bricks and to mix mortar and to work in the fields.... Moses and Aaron went to Pharaoh and said, "This is what the LORD, the God of Israel says: 'Let my people go so that they may hold a festival to me' ... But the King of Egypt said ... 'Why are you taking the people away from their labour? Get back to your work!'"' (Exodus 1:14 CEV and 5:1–4).

23. Rob Bell and Don Golden, *Jesus Wants to Save Christians: A Manifesto for the Church in Exile* (Grand Rapids, Mich.: Zondervan, 2008), 32.

24. See also incidents found in Mark chapters 2 and 3; Matthew 12; Luke 13 and 14 and in John 5, 7 and 9.

25. Stephen Westerholm, 'Sabbath', in Joel B. Green, ed., et al., *Dictionary of Jesus and the Gospels* (Downers Grove, Ill.: InterVarsity, 1992), 719.

26. For more on the philosophical theories about ethics, see the 'For Further Reading' list.

27. Stanley Hauerwas, *The Peaceable Kingdom: A Primer in Christian Ethics* (South Bend, Ind.: University of Notre Dame, 1983), 95.

28. Eric Williams, *Capitalism and Slavery* (Chapel Hill, N.C.: University of North Carolina, 1994), 42.

29. See, for example, Exodus 21:20; Leviticus 25:44; Ephesians 6:5; Colossians 3:22; 4:1; 1 Timothy 6:1; Titus 2:9.

30. Cited in Steve Chalke and Alan Mann, *The Lost Message of Jesus* (Grand Rapids: Zondervan, 2003), 54.

31. Karl Barth, *Church Dogmatics,* vol. 2 (London: Continuum International, 2000), 284.

32. See also Psalm 30:5; 86:15; 145:8–9.

33. See Genesis 5:24: 6:9, Isaiah 1:11–14; Amos 5:21–23 or Micah 6:8.

34. See Acts 9:2; 19:9, 23; 22:4; 24:14, 22.

35. Hauerwas and Willimon, *Resident Aliens*, 51.

36. Richard Lischer, 'The Sermon on the Mount as Radical Pastoral Care', *Interpretation* 41 (1987), 1:161–62.

37. Seth Godin, 'Tribes: We Need You to Lead Us', *RSA Journal* (Summer 2009).

38. Alasdair MacIntyre, *After Virtue* (King's Lynn, Norfolk: Biddles, 2004), 216.

39. Marvin R. Wilson, *Our Father Abraham: Jewish Roots of the Christian Faith* (Grand Rapids, Mich.: Eerdmans, 1989), 150.

40. Samuel Wells, *Improvisation: The Drama of Christian Ethics* (London: SPCK, 2004), 76–77.

41. Kenneth E. Bailey, *Jesus through Middle Eastern Eyes* (Downers Grove, Ill.: InterVarsity, 2008), 292–93.

42. William C. Spohn, *Go and Do Likewise: Jesus and Ethics* (New York: Continuum, 2003), 89.

43. Joel B. Green, *The Gospel of Luke* (Grand Rapids, Mich.: Eerdmans, 1997), 426.

44. Keep remembering that the 'kingdom of heaven' is Jesus' way of speaking about the rule of Yahweh, here and now, rather than a reference to some future home beyond the stars!

45. See, for instance, Luke 2:40; 3:22; 4:1, 14, 16–18.

46. For more on this, see Alan Mann, *A Permanent Becoming: A Contemporary Look at the Fruit of the Spirit* (Colorado Springs: Authentic, 2008).

47. Wells, *Improvisation*, 75.

48. Ibid.

49. *Evan Almighty*, Universal Studios, 2007.

50. N. T. Wright, *Matthew for Everyone: Chapters 1 to 15* (Louisville, Ky.: Westminster/John Knox, 2004), 36.

51. The Torah, or Written Law, is the foundation of the Jewish Scriptures, traditionally handed down to (and written by) Moses by God at Mt Sinai and revered as the most important document in Judaism. The Torah consists of the five books of Genesis, Exodus, Leviticus, Numbers and Deuteronomy, detailing the grand sweep of Jewish history that covers creation, promise, the giving of the Law and the march into the Promised Land.

52. All of these laws, and far more, were found on various sites by doing an Internet search.

53. Spohn, *Go and Do Likewise*, 31.

54. Cited in Chalke and Mann, *Lost Message of Jesus*, 87.

55. See, for example, Matthew 3:2; 4:23; 9:35; 11:12; 12:28, etc.

56. See Matthew 4:12–24.

57. Hauerwas and Willimon, *Resident Aliens*, 84.

58. Ibid., 73.

59. There has been a huge movement in Western European culture away from religion towards spirituality. Organised religion is distrusted and discredited. Many people, including growing numbers of once-faithful churchgoers, view Christianity as a religious institution and reject it. They are searching for spiritual nourishment – for the liberation of a lifestyle rather than the straitjacket of an organised religion. Spirituality has become disassociated from the idea of religion. For centuries, religion

was a joined-up system of beliefs and practices that provided a framework for every sphere of life. Around the beginning of the twentieth century, driven largely by the rise of psychoanalysis, a tension developed between the growing exploration of personal religious experience and the recognised categories of institutional religion. By the end of the twentieth century, many people considered institutional religion to be unbearably restrictive and outmoded. An individual's private belief structure and personal experience, which they had to be free to interpret and act upon in a way that 'released' rather than 'bound' them, was now seen as paramount. Spirituality had effectively declared independence from religion and was now free to take on any form we felt right and true. Religion had become associated with strict ideas and arcane practices, irrelevant rules and rituals, fundamentalist beliefs and teachings. For many, if not most people, when they use the word *religion*, they are conjuring with ideas that have been associated with religion since the early thirteenth century. (The word is derived from the Anglo-French *religiun*, meaning 'a reverence for and contemplation of God', usually within the institution of the church, through the practice of time-honoured rites and rituals.) Under the heavy weight of tradition, all too often this 'religion' becomes narrow and legalistic, stifling individual expression and encounter, curtailing spiritual growth and faith development, setting over-restrictive boundaries, shunning innovation, resisting cultural shifts and felt needs and insisting on a one-size-fits-all, take-it-or-leave-it, teacher-led learning straitjacket. Religion is then viewed as a set of rules – do this, don't do that – used to disconnect yourself from various behaviours and people to achieve divine approval. Before the thirteenth century, however, it had an altogether different definition. The English word *religion* derives from the Latin *ligare*, meaning 'to bind or connect'. It was prefixed with *re* (again) to form *religare* – reconnect. Religion in its origins was far from being about disconnection, referring instead to reconnection to God, to yourself, to others, to community and to creation. It was about a *calling to* something, rather than a *calling away*. True religion is a guide and aid to spirituality rather than a stumbling block in its way.

60. The right to put people to death had been taken away from the Jewish people by the Romans. This is something that is seen again in all the religious and political to and fro that surrounded Jesus' execution. 'Pilate told them, "Take him and judge him by your own laws." The crowd replied, "We are not allowed to put anyone to death"' (John 18:31 CEV).

61. Bailey, *Jesus through Middle Eastern Eyes*, 234.

62. Ibid.

63. George W. Stroup, *The Promise of Narrative Theology: Recovering the Gospel in the Church* (Louisville, Ky.: John Knox, 1981), 111.

64. Neil Messer, *Christian Ethics* (Louisville, Ky.: Presbyterian Publishing Corp., 2006), 133.

65. Hauerwas and Willimon, *Resident Aliens*, 53.

66. Walter Brueggemann, *The Prophetic Imagination* (Minneapolis: Fortress, 2001), 95.

67. Alan Storkey, *Jesus and Politics: Confronting the Powers* (Grand Rapids, Mich.: Baker/Brazos, 2005).

68. Hauerwas and Willimon, *Resident Aliens*, 47.

69. Hauerwas, *The Peaceable Kingdom*, 1.

70. There is for the Church a huge difference between whether an action is believed to be right or wrong according to the cultural norms of a society and whether an action actually is right or wrong. This is the difference between a culturally subjective relativism and the church's affirmation that, in Yahweh's universe, truth is objective – that though it might not be universally agreed, there is, in fact, an ethic for the whole universe.

71. See Ruth Benedict, *Patterns of Culture* (New York: Mariner, 2005 [1934]).

72. See Alasdair MacIntyre, *After Virtue: A Study in Moral Theory* (South Bend, Ind.: University of Notre Dame Press, 1984).

73. *Christendom* is the name given to the culture that has dominated European society from around the eleventh century until the end of the twentieth. For more on this, see Stuart Murray, *Church After Christendom* (Carlisle, Cumbria: Paternoster, 2005).

74. Robert Jensen, cited in Stuart Murray, *Post-Christendom: Church and Mission in a Strange New World*, (Carlisle, Cumbria: Paternoster, 2004), 18.

75. For more on this, see Mark E. Biddle, *Missing the Mark: Sin and Its Consequences in Biblical Theology* (Nashville: Abingdon, 2005).

76. Lesslie Newbigin, Lamin Sanneh, and Jenny Taylor, cited in Steve Chalke, *One God*, (East Sussex: Spring Harvest, 2005), 61.

77. Newbigin, Sanneh, and Taylor, in Chalke, *One God*, 61.

78. *About a Boy*, Universal Studios (DVD, 2003).

79. Richard Koch and Chris Smith, *Suicide of the West* (London: Continuum, 2006), 145.

80. Pete Lowman, *A Long Way East of Eden: Could God Explain the Mess We're In?* (Carlisle, Cumbria: Paternoster, 2006), 257

81. Brian McLaren, *Finding Our Way Again* (Nashville: Nelson, 2008), 124–25.

82. See Michael Polanyi, *Personal Knowledge: Towards a Post-Critical Philosophy* (Chicago: University of Chicago, 1974).

83. McLaren, *Finding Our Way Again*, 125.

84. Hauerwas and Willimon, *Resident Aliens*, 102.

85. Ibid., 138.

86. Ibid., 94.

87. Ibid., 65.

88. See Exodus 13:8 and Deuteronomy 6:7.

89. Charles F. Melchert, *Wise Teaching: Biblical Wisdom and Educational Ministry* (London: Continuum, 1998), 269.

90. Ibid., 10.

91. Melchert, *Wise Teaching,* 269

92. Rob Bell and Don Golden, *Jesus Wants to Save Christians: A Manifesto for the Church in Exile* (Grand Rapids, Mich.: Zondervan, 2008), 180.

93. General Omar N. Bradley, from a speech given on November 11, 1948.

94. Karl Barth, *Church Dogmatics* (London: T. & T. Clark, 2004), 4.3.2.

95. Christendom is the name given to the culture that has dominated European society from around the eleventh century until the end of the twentieth.

96. James D. Berkley, *Essential Christianity: Finding the God Who Loves You* (Grand Rapids, Mich.: Zondervan, 2001), 10.

97. Graham Cray, cited in Gerard Kelly, *Sing the Lord's Song in a Strange Land*, (East Sussex: Spring Harvest, 2004), 24.

98. Kenneth Leech, *Through Our Long Exile: Contextual Theology and the Urban Experience* (Maryknoll, N.Y.: Orbis, 2002), 229.

99. A phrase made popular by Stanley Hauerwas and William Willimon through their book of the same name.

100. David Smith, *Mission After Christendom* (London: Darton Longman and Todd, 2003), 44.

101. David Bebbington, 'Evangelicals, Theology and Social Transformation', in *Movement for Change: Evangelical Perspectives on Social Transformation*, David Hilborn, ed. (Carlisle, Cumbria: Paternoster, 2004), 10.

102. Hauerwas and Willimon, *Resident Aliens*, 95.

103. Ibid., 123.

104. The state finds it just as hard to give up certain benefits of Christendom as the Church does.

105. Ajith Fernando, cited in Kelly, *Sing The Lord's Song in a Strange Land*, 103.

106. Hauerwas and Willimon, *Resident Aliens*, 46.

107. Gerard Kelly, *Spring Harvest* 2005.

108. The famous quote, based on the theme of Niemöller's sermon, and others he gave around the same time, about the inactivity of the German Church as well as the silence of the country's intellectuals following the Nazi rise to power, was first published after the war in 1955: 'First they came for the Communists, and I didn't speak up, because I wasn't a Communist. Then they came for the Jews, and I didn't speak up, because I wasn't a Jew. Then they came for the Catholics, and I didn't speak up, because I was a Protestant. Then they came for me, and by that time there was no one left to speak up for me.'

109. In his book *On Secular Authority*, Martin Luther had taught that God rules the earthly kingdom through secular government, by means of law (that is, the sword or compulsion) and the heavenly kingdom (that is, Christians insofar as they are a new creation) through grace. Civil government's role is simply to keep outward peace in society. It has no business enforcing spiritual laws. 'The laws of worldly government extend no further than to life and property and what is external upon earth.'

110. Messer, *Christian Ethics*, 135.

111. In many ways, this is a residual of Christendom conditioning.

112. Perhaps the only passage that even comes close is Exodus 21:22–25, which reads: 'If men who are fighting hit a pregnant woman and she gives birth prematurely but there is no serious injury, the offender must be fined whatever the woman's husband demands and the court allows. But if there is serious injury, you are to take life for life, eye for eye, tooth for tooth, hand for hand, foot for foot, burn for burn, wound for wound, bruise for bruise' 'Serious injury' (Hebrew *ason*) in the above verse may well include injury to both the mother and child.

113. *Didache* (meaning 'teaching') or, to give it its full name 'The Teaching of the Lord to the Gentiles by the Twelve Apostles', is an early 'handbook' of ethical instruction and sets out various spiritual disciplines, or what could be described as Rules of Life. Scholars agree that parts of it were probably in existence as early as the first few decades after Pentecost and that it had been edited together into a standard format by the late first or very early second century. The Didache was widely circulated in early Christian communities and was considered by some of the Church Fathers as part of what we would now call the Canon, though eventually it was not accepted into the New Testament (with the exception of the Ethiopian Orthodox Church).

114. Hauerwas and Willimon, *Resident Aliens*, 80.

115. The book is still in print! Charles Sheldon, *In His Steps: What Would Jesus Do?* (Alachua, Fla.: Bridge-Logos, 2000).

116. Gotthold Lessing, from his essay 'On the Proof of the Spirit and of Power'.

117. N. T. Wright, *The Challenge of Jesus* (Downers Grove, Ill.: InterVarsity, 1999), 1.

118. Hauerwas and Willimon, *Resident Aliens*, 55.

119. Spohn, *Go and Do Likewise*, 9.

120. Bill Hybels, *Too Busy Not to Pray: Slowing Down to Be with God* (Downers Grove, Ill.: InterVarsity, 2008), 99.

121. Jonathan R. Wilson, *Gospel Virtues: Practicing Faith, Hope, and Love in Uncertain Times* (Eugene, Ore.: Wipf and Stock, 2004), 25.

122. Spohn, *Go and Do Likewise*, 29.

123. *Eschatology* – from the Greek *eschatos*, meaning 'last', and – *logy*, meaning 'the study of'. Eschatology is the part of theology concerned with the ultimate destiny of humanity. Christian and Jewish eschatologies view the end times as the consummation or perfection of God's creation of the universe.

124. This is in stark contrast to the Utilitarian ethics of Jeremy Bentham, the famous English philosopher, social reformer and father of utilitarianism (see Part one, section 1) who articulated what is known as the 'greatest-happiness principle'. This defines 'happiness' as the maximization of pleasure and the minimization of pain. Bentham held that one should always act so as to produce the 'the greatest good for the greatest number of people'. Therefore, he and John Stuart Mill taught that the basis for the desirability of any action comes down to the 'net amount of happiness it brings; the number of people it brings it to, and the duration of that happiness'.

125. Adapted from an idea originally written by my friend Dave Steell.

for further reading

Ethics is a complex subject, and there are limits to what can be achieved within the confines of one small book. So, for all those interested in understanding more, here are some books worth looking at, though please be aware that some of them are very academic in nature.

Bowie, Robert A. *Ethical Studies* (Cheltenham: Nelson Thornes, 2001).

Brown, William P., ed. *Character and Scripture: Moral Formation, Community and Biblical Interpretation*. Grand Rapids, Mich.: Eerdmans, 2002.

Burridge, Richard A. *Imitating Jesus: An Inclusive Approach to New Testament Ethics*. Grand Rapids, Mich.: Eerdmans, 2007.

Disbrey, Claire. *Living in Grace: Virtue Ethics and Christian Living*. Oxford: Bible Reading Fellowship, 2007.

Gill, Robin, ed. *The Cambridge Companion to Christian Ethics*. Cambridge: Cambridge University Press, 2001.

Hauerwas, Stanley, and Samuel Wells, eds. *The Blackwell Companion to Christian Ethics*. Oxford: Blackwell, 2006.

Hauerwas, Stanley. *The Peaceable Kingdom: A Primer in Christian Ethics*. London: SCM, 1983.

Hauerwas, Stanley, and William H. Willimon. *Resident Aliens*. Nashville: Abingdon, 1989.

Hays, Richard. *The Moral Vision of the New Testament*. Edinburgh: Clark, 1996.

Kotva, Joseph J. *The Christian Case for Virtue Ethics*. Washington, D.C.: Georgetown University Press, 1996.

Kunhiyop, Samuel Waje. *African Christian Ethics*. Nairobi, Kenya: Hippo Books, 2008.

MacIntyre, Alasdair. *After Virtue*. King's Lynn: Biddles, 2004.

Messer, Neil. *Christian Ethics*. London: SCM Press, 2006.

Mitchell, Craig Vincent. *Charts of Christian Ethics*. Grand Rapids, Mich.: Zondervan, 2006.

Oliphant, Jill. *Religious Ethics for AS and A2*. London: Routledge, 2007.

Rae, Scott. *Moral Choices: An Introduction to Ethics*. Grand Rapids, Mich.: Zondervan, 2009.

Rosenstand, Nina. *The Moral of the Story*. New York: McGraw-Hill, 2000.

Sloane, Andrew. *At Home in a Strange Land: Using the Old Testament in Christian Ethics*. Peabody: Hendrickson, 2008.

Spohn, William C. *Go and Do Likewise*. New York: Continuum, 2003.

Stassen, Glen H., and David P. Gushee. *Kingdom Ethics: Following Jesus in Contemporary Context*. Downers Grove, Ill.: InterVarsity Academic, 2003.

Stott, John R. W., and John Wyatt. *Issues Facing Christians Today*. Grand Rapids, Mich.: Zondervan, 2006.

Vardy, Peter, and Paul Grosch. *The Puzzle of Ethics*. London: Fount, 1999.

Wells, Samuel. *Improvisation: The Drama of Christian Ethics*. London: SPCK, 2004.

Wilson, Jonathan R. *Gospel Virtues: Practicing Faith, Hope, and Love in Uncertain Times*. Downers Grove, Ill.: InterVarsity, 1998.